# Mom, Dad ...

# Can We Talk?

# Mom, Dad ...
# Can We Talk?

*Insight and Perspectives to Help Us Do
What's Best for Our Aging Parents*

DICK EDWARDS

**Retired Mayo Clinic Eldercare Specialist**

With Mike Ransom and Ruth Weispfenning

*Mom, Dad ... Can We Talk? Insight and Perspectives to Help Us Do What's Best for Our Aging Parents*

The stories in *Mom, Dad ... Can We Talk?* are from real life experiences, but names have been changed.

Published by Wheatmark®
610 East Delano Street, Suite 104
Tucson, Arizona 85705 U.S.A.
www.wheatmark.com

International Standard Book Number: 978-1-60494-240-8
Library of Congress Control Number: 2008943799

Front cover photo by Tim Worthington.
Author photo by Tom Dube.

*Each of us is someone's child;*
*many of us have parents living;*
*and all of us should have an older person in our life*
*to share with, learn from, and care for.*

—Dick Edwards

*To our parents and our children
and all from whom we have learned*

# CONTENTS

Welcome! As you read we ask you to:
*stop and think,*
*evaluate,*
*anticipate,*
*communicate,*
*navigate,* and
*celebrate* your parents' growing older.

# SETTING THE STAGE

During my thirty-five-year career in older adult services, I was privileged to share in the lives of hundreds of older people. I formed supportive relationships with them and their families. I was called upon daily to offer support and counsel.

As I reflect on my experiences, I have concluded that adult children generally have good intentions, but they are often ill prepared to make the best of relationships with their parents, to manage the myriad of issues that are common to the later years in family life, and to maximize the opportunities for good times. Over and over I heard adult children say, "I feel a responsibility for my parents. I care. I want to do the right thing. What is the right thing? I welcome help."

*Mom, Dad ... Can We Talk?* is my response to their pleas. It draws from my years of working with older people and shares insights about how adult children and their families can manage the challenges and get the most out of the final years with their parents. I share the personal stories of many, including lessons from a survey I conducted of one hundred adult children who are on—or who have recently completed—the journey with their older parents. Numerous quotes from those responding to the survey appear in callout boxes throughout the book.

The Pew Research Center estimates that seventy-seven million baby boomers, the sandwich generation, are simultaneously dealing with their own life issues, the needs of their children, and the needs of an elderly parent or parents. I've written this book for them.

For some families, this stage of life—when parents grow old—is a walk in the park. Relationships are tidy, everyone communicates, resources are available, choices are sufficient, decisions come easy, and the later years are golden. For other families, maybe for most, these years are characterized by fear of the unknown and frustration: fear of what's to happen, fear of failure, fear of not doing the right thing, and, frustration with parents, siblings, and the system. It's a draining push-pull that taps and saps time, energy, and resources. These are uncharted waters.

There are many references, guides, and compendiums available—clinical and encyclopedic in nature—that help adult children help their aging parents. Much of this information resides on the Internet. Google the phrases "living will," "healthcare directive," or "nursing homes in Minnesota," for example, and you'll see long lists of sources that provide information about the topics. Some information, though, the personal and practical things you really need to know, aren't easily found. It's difficult to search the Internet for "How do I get my siblings to share the work in caring for

Mom?" or "How can I convince Dad it's time to give up driving?" My book addresses these situations. It's foundational, fundamental. Read it first and then seek out the other information as required.

*Mom, Dad ... Can We Talk?* looks at roles and relationships among family members. It acknowledges and respects family history to help gauge present-day expectations. It identifies areas of potential difficulty as well as areas of potential pleasure. It asks you to stop and think, to anticipate, and to start the conversations with your parents and those who care about them.

I asked my colleagues Ruth Weispfenning and Mike Ransom to help me write this book. Ruth is a licensed social worker and director of resident services at the retirement community where I served as administrator. She is a talented problem-solving coach. Time and again I watched Ruth calmly guide families through stress-filled situations. Mike is a memoirist who has written over a dozen books. He has the gift of asking questions, listening, gently probing, and then translating what he hears and learns into written words. He has a special fondness for older people, and he delights in helping them tell their life stories for family and friends to treasure forever.

We tried to make *Mom, Dad ... Can We Talk?* an enjoyable, reassuring read about topics common to a stage in family life and often challenging to manage. Take pleasure in the stories and insights we share, but most important, find in them things you can draw from as you share this time with parents and older persons in your life. It's all worth it in the end.

# 1

# CURTAIN UP ON ACT 3!

Imagine you and your family in a three-act play. Act 1 features your growing up years. It's a fun time, safe and predictable. Your parents are central to your universe. Siblings and friends, relatives and neighbors, teachers and coaches round out the cast. It's a time for learning, growing, and becoming. Family roles and relationships are formed. Personal and family foundations are laid.

Act 2 spotlights your young adult years when you are consumed with completing your education, starting a family, and embarking on your career. Siblings move from the nest and see one another much less often than in Act 1: at holidays, weddings, baptisms, and funerals. Your parents, while not incidental to your hectic life, are there, participating, but they are on their own and rarely share center stage.

Before you know it, the curtain lifts on Act 3. You've become middle-aged. The cast of characters has changed. Some have gone; others have joined. At the start of this act, you look over your shoulder and say, "Who's that over there? Oh my

> *"What is difficult as an adult child is not knowing what the future holds for my parents. What's going to happen next that we will need to face together? I fear the phone's ringing. I feel like I'm living on the edge of something dreadful."*

God, it's my parents. Where have they been? They can't be in their eighties, can they? Have I been that engrossed? What have I missed?"

The close-knit family in Act 1 that diluted somewhat in Act 2 must now regroup in Act 3 to grow older with their parents.

The probability for your success in your family's Act 3 boils down to how well you and your family anticipate needs, educate yourselves, communicate and delegate, navigate the issues and opportunities you come upon, and learn to celebrate the simple things in life with your parents. Many families do these things well, with relative ease, while others have to work a bit harder.

We assume the curtain is up on Act 3 of your family play. For many families, this act can be a glorious climax to lives well lived. For some, it may be a regrettable close to what could have been. We've written this book to help you achieve the former.

> *"Those last years were challenging at times, but we took them head-on. My, what joys we shared."*

We know that children learn by example. Your children are watching you, taking mental notes as they see you interact with your aging parents. What they observe and experience will set the stage when you are the aging parent in Act 3, twenty or thirty years from now.

Our hope is that as you read *Mom, Dad ... Can We Talk?* you will first stop and think and then start the dialogue. We want thunderous applause to accompany the curtain closing on Act 3 of your family play. Bravo!

# 2

# GROWING OLDER
# HAPPENS

Growing older happens. We are born; we grow old; we die. This cycle has been repeating itself since Adam and Eve, so we invite you to accept and celebrate that fact. Growing older is part of life itself, and there are physiological and genetic aspects that one can't do much about. In spite of the many books on the market about the subject, in spite of all the Madison Avenue hype promoting a wrinkle cream or an anti-aging potion or lotion that slows the process, growing older inevitably happens.

Many of our parents enjoy active, independent lives. However, all of us must sooner or later come to grips with the reality that our parents are growing older; that in doing so they may well experience the loss of loved ones, health, stamina, independence; and that ultimately they will die. As

> *"I noticed when my parents stopped trying to stay young, they began to enjoy growing older."*

we do with most troubling thoughts in life, we push them into the far corner of our mind.

Though the aging process hasn't changed much, what has changed is that with every year we live longer on average. The current life expectancy for adults in the United States is 79.9 years, which means your parents have a 50 percent chance of living into their eighties and beyond. Therefore, each year more of us in the sandwich generation (those caring for their aging parents while supporting their own children) will be living longer with parents in their eighties and nineties.

My coauthors and I are not experts in the physiological aspects of growing older. What we do know, though, is that you do not need to fear the process of your parents growing older. Don't bemoan it. Those who have been denied the privilege of having older parents—through illness or accident—would gladly trade places with you. Your growing-older parents are a gift. Celebrate them!

Unless your parents die suddenly in their prime, they and you are probably going to experience some degree of difficulty in this process. For some it will be health; for others it will be loss. Loss of body functions, and the personal humiliation that goes with it. Loss of independence. Loss of sense of place. The point is that unless they die suddenly, you're probably not going to escape some of this.

We are not soft-pedaling the fact that growing older can be difficult. Our friend Lois, experiencing all that came with being eighty-nine, summed it up nicely by saying, "We're all just trying to endure the indignities of aging as gracefully as we can." Are you listening? The challenge to the kids is to help their parents do this gracefully and with dignity.

The media paint such a negative picture of growing older and play on our fears of nursing homes. A TV ad shows a young, attractive daughter sitting and holding hands with her dad on the front steps of his porch. The ad touts a new medication for treating mild forms of dementia. The daughter says, "I was so afraid I would have to put Dad in a nursing home."

There they go, playing the "Heaven forbid the nursing home" card. If her father needs to be in a nursing home, he needs to be in a nursing home. Some little pill won't stop it from happening.

When a family begins dealing with an aging parent, they typically know only two extremes: care at home and care in a nursing home. There are many options in between—and by the way, nursing homes as we know them today won't be the same in the not-too-distant future. They are being transformed. They will have a changed role in the continuum of care and services. Older people will enter nursing homes, if at all, at a later age and for a shorter stay.

Most of us don't sit around the dinner table with our parents and talk about aging and dying. Death seems to be a taboo family topic saved for the bedside as a parent takes his or her last breath in intensive care. We've learned that seniors are much more comfortable with the topic than we expected. Older persons are often asked if they have written end-of-life wishes: do they wish to be resuscitated, do they wish to be intubated, which family

> *"As Mom slowed down, we set our sights to the level of activity we thought she could handle, and it was enough to help keep her engaged."*

members to contact, which funeral home they prefer. While these may seem like awkward questions to ask, nearly everyone will respond, "Oh, we've already contacted the funeral home, and everything's in place." You can bet that your parents have done quite a bit of thinking about their dying, and they probably are more accepting of it than you are. It's just that they haven't shared many of their thoughts about it with you. Take a lead from your parents and don't feel timid about the topic of their dying.

Now that we've reminded you of the obvious—that everyone dies and that growing older can be fraught with difficulties—let's put those thoughts aside. Dying and despair are not our main themes. Instead, let's talk about *life* and *family relationships.* We want to help you make the most of your time with your parents.

After living with hundreds of seniors through their later years, we admit that we don't fully understand or appreciate the aging process. Yes, it is rough getting older. But what most people do is reach back, apply the coping skills and life experiences they've had, and basically make the best of growing older.

> *"One of their joys while growing older was watching their children become wholesome, productive adults."*

Some are naturally better than others at doing this. Some have always been able to roll with the punches. People who have a history of coping with adversity and toughing things out might view aging as just another challenge. "I've marched up to this sort of thing before," they'll say, "and I'm sure I'll do quite nicely, thank you." We've learned that nearly everyone experiences aging just differently enough that we need to respect each variation.

Aging provides chances for people to shine. Some seniors come alive in their twilight years and show a different side. As evidenced in the following story, kids are surprised to see what Mom can do on her own now that Dad's gone.

*An adult daughter worried that her mother would curl in a corner and crumble after her husband died. Instead, she was soon planning a cruise to the Caribbean. The daughter reported to her friends, "Mother just called to ask if I could stop by her apartment to help her choose which bathing suit to take on her upcoming cruise. And she surprised me even more by asking, "Oh by the way, would you be willing to join me?"*

We've seen so many families share the ups and downs of aging and laugh and enjoy their way through their parents' later years. There will be challenges, but the times can be enriching and fun. Families, realizing that they don't have an unlimited amount of time left with Mom and Dad, often deal with issues that have been on the table for years.

They bury hatchets. In one family, the mother and daughter, who had not spoken for twenty years, restarted their relationship with a brief visit while the mother was in a nursing home. Nobody ever knew why they had stopped speaking.

They come to peace about an important issue in their lives, such as never having told the nieces and nephews that their mother had been married once before.

They no longer are shy about saying "I love you" when they meet or depart.

At some point in their lives, adult children realize that regardless of how well they *like* their mother or father, they should still *respect* them. The teachings and writings of the world's religions and faith traditions nearly all speak to the important role of the elderly.

Finally, since "it happens," one must keep living until "it does," as Sophie firmly believed:

> *Sophie was a delightful lady with a loving husband. She had terminal breast cancer and had come to the nursing home to die. Her condition stabilized shortly after she came in, so she began planning a vacation. The nursing staff asked the administrator to talk with Sophie about the denial of her illness. As he began a discussion with Sophie, she looked at him and said, "I know I am dying, but I plan to live until I die." Sophie didn't live long enough to take that vacation, but she provided a powerful lesson on living with a positive attitude.*

---

**Put down this book. Call your parents.**

# 3

# SEEK FIRST TO UNDERSTAND

Adult children need to pause a moment in their rush-here and rush-there lives to put themselves in their parents' shoes. As with many situations, the key to helping a parent grow older is to seek first to understand. Yes, the fifth of Stephen Covey's *Seven Habits of Highly Effective People* also applies to living with growing-older parents. Empathy is key. Genuinely try to imagine what it's like for your parent. Try your best to see the world through your mom or dad's eyes. Educate yourself so that you can gauge expectations and find your role.

Can you possibly imagine what it would be like to be eighty-five? Imagine a cataract in your eye, a hearing aid in your ear, corns on your feet, a bladder that you can't trust—to feel and experience yourself as old. What would it be

> *"The older I become, the better I understand what my mother's going through."*

like to have siblings and lifelong friends, business associates, a spouse, and neighbors die one by one as you live on. How would you feel if you could no longer drive? Or if you fell in the shower and could not help yourself up?

> *"As their health failed, I began to feel more like a parent to my parents, and I realized the roles were reversing."*

First of all, don't pretend you know anything about being eighty-five. And when you become that age, your eighty-five will be different than your parents' eighty-fives. How you experience it and manage it is shaped by years of behaviors, coping skills, expectations, and genetic makeup. For some it's a snap; for others it's a grueling, uphill climb. So, the point is, don't generalize.

> *When Phil's eighty-year-old father laments, "It's tough getting older," Phil tries never to respond, "I know how you feel." Phil has experienced many things in his life, but he has no idea what waking up one morning in an eighty-year-old body feels like either physically or emotionally.*
>
> *Phil also has no idea what emotions set in when his father realizes that he has a finite (and few) number of times to enjoy what means most to him. "My gosh, this could be my last Thanksgiving with my family." Or, "Spring is my favorite time of year. How many more will I be able to enjoy in this house?"*

When a parent says, "It's tough getting older," you have an opportunity to say, "Tell me about it. I have no idea, but maybe I could learn something from what you're going through." Then listen quietly and compassionately to what they have to say. They aren't necessarily looking for you to solve their problems. They may simply want someone with whom to share their thoughts. Don't rush to try to make growing older what you think might be easier for them—or something it's not. Your dad may not be what you remember him as. So understand where he's at today. You may see that he has changed, or at a minimum sees things differently.

Empathizing with your parents builds a good foundation for the insights we will share in the remainder of this book. Your parents will be more receptive to your involvement in their growing-older process when they see that you're listening and trying to see things from their perspective. You really don't know much about what they're going through, so be cautious about giving too much advice too soon.

*Reflect on the losses your parents are experiencing.*
*Ask yourself, How would I feel?*

# 4

# Some Things Never Change

In the beginning were our parents, and our parents had us, and we became family. We start our life surrounded by the joys of family, and if we play our cards right, we end our life surrounded by the joys of family. In between those times, whether we have good, bad, or neutral family experiences growing up, they lay the groundwork for how we will be and who we become. At some point, we leave our family and go to college, join the military, marry, move to another town, and start our first job, start our own families. Over time, the *physical* relationships with our family change—how far we live from home, what we do, how often we return to visit, how often we see our siblings—but the dynamic,

> *"I know this is true: Parents never stop being parents. While circumstances may have changed and roles may have reversed, I'm still the child and must let Dad be the parent. It's what I'll want, too."*

engrained *emotional* relationships we have within our family typically don't change.

We stated at the beginning of the book that we can liken our years with our family to a three-act play.

Let's assume in Act 1, which covers your childhood years at home, the audience sees that Mom is goodhearted but has a dominant personality. They observe that Dad is a hard worker but passive; sister Sarah is the kindest person on earth; brother Larry is a jerk; and that Mom and Dad like sister Julie the best; she can do no wrong in their eyes.

Act 2 covers your young adult years, which fly by, and before we know it the curtain rises on Act 3. The audience sees the same cast of characters as in Acts 1 and 2, but that, though older, Mom is still a dominant-but-goodhearted mom; Dad may not be quite as hardworking, but he's still passive; Larry is still a jerk; Sarah is still wonderful; and Julie is still the chosen child—just as they were in Acts 1 and 2. Life simply works that way, so it's best to acknowledge that relationships exhibited in Act 1 of your family play, like them or not, will probably be there in Act 3. While we do believe we are capable of change, there is truth in the adage, *some things never change.*

> *"I think being the oldest child I was looked upon to take care of things."*

We are time and again baffled when we see families ignoring this fact. They expect things from family members that they have never before shown competence in doing or an interest in doing. The son who has always been short of money may not be the best person to become power of attorney. Why should the daughter whose house is a cluttered mess be entrusted to organize the move to assisted living? She isn't capable of doing so. Why, now, in their parents' later years, would families expect members to shine in an area in which they never excelled before?

Each of us begins Act 3 of our family drama with the good baggage and the bad baggage of our family history. We must deal with that baggage, because acknowledging our family for who we are and what we are builds the foundation for dealing with the issues and opportunities of our aging parents.

The following conversation among four adult children, each a highly successful businessman, shows their reluctance to tell Mom it's time for her to move from independent to assisted living. Though they love their mom, they know she doesn't like to hear unpleasant news. They will always be their mother's little boys.

*"You tell her," says one.*

*"No, you tell her," adds the second.*

*"I'm not telling her," declares the third.*

*"Don't look at me," pleads the fourth.*

*These are not four little boys arguing about who should tell their mom that they just broke the garage window. These are four grown men, brothers, each immensely successful in adult life, titans of industry and commerce. Yet, when it comes time to tell their mother she must move from her independent living apartment to an assisted living room because she needs reminders about her medications and assistance getting dressed, they become cowering wimps.*

*They vigorously debate who should break the news.*

*"You're the oldest. It should come from you. She's always respected your opinion over ours."*

*"Are you crazy? She'll bite my head off. The last thing I'm going to do is walk into her apartment and tell her we're moving her out. She still tells me to keep my elbows off the table and to chew with my mouth closed."*

Parents tend to value the opinion of their eldest, no matter what. In the following story told by an adult child from a family of six children, Einar, rather than Eleanor, will be consulted for his opinion, simply because he's the oldest.

*Growing up we were a close-knit family—three brothers, three sisters, mom and dad. We were a farm family of the classic Norwegian Lutheran tradition. Everyone worked hard and contributed to family life. Einar was the oldest. Mother thought he could do no wrong. Sometimes we wondered if he could do anything right. (Just kidding, Einar.)*

*Brother Einar took over the family farm and worked alongside Dad. As adults we remained close-knit, returning to the family farm often and gladly for holidays and any occasion we could deem special. Mother was the spirit, the glue.*

*After Dad died and Mother's health began to fail, she became the primary focus of family concern. She had complicated health issues. Our single sister, Eleanor, had a profession related to caring for older people, so she became the family equivalent of 911 when it came to Mother and her needs. Eleanor did everything.*

*For months and months Eleanor monitored Mother's situation, coordinated and orchestrated. She talked with the doctors, the social workers, and the array of healthcare professionals trying to help our mother. Eleanor researched the options, reviewed them all with Mother, and communicated thoroughly and faithfully with the rest of us. She was the go-to person who helped us understand and do the right thing. We did what Eleanor asked.*

*Everyone greatly appreciated Eleanor. She and Mother grew closer. Eleanor made certain*

*Mother maintained her dignity and her pivotal role in the family. Mother still ran things from her room in the nursing home and still presided at family gatherings on the farm.*

*When Eleanor and Mother met with the surgeons to discuss the crucial matter of leg amputation because of complications from diabetes, Mother listened carefully, thoughtfully pondered each option and its consequences.*

*With the ever-faithful Eleanor at her side, the doctor assured Mother that it would have to be her decision. Rather than turning to Eleanor, Mother turned to the surgeon and said, "I'll have to see what Einar has to say. He's the eldest, you know."*

No discussion about family dynamics surrounding concerns and care for the aging parent would be complete without mention of the out-of-town sibling. Here's what Keith, an adult child who lives far from his parents, has to say:

*For years my sister and her family enjoyed the benefits of proximity and ease of access to our parents. She and they lived in the same city. Mother and Dad attended all the grandchildren's school and church programs, Little League games, music recitals, birthday gatherings, prom nights, and graduations. They were tightly woven into the daily fabric of my sister's family life. I was envious. I lived 210 miles away with my family, and our trips home were infrequent and generally associated with holiday celebrations or family funerals. As our parents grew older and their needs for support and care increased, my sister, the sibling living closest, became the twenty-four/seven caregiving daughter. I, the out-of-town sibling, was no longer envious.*

How best then to play the role of out-of-town sibling? Some have been known to blow in, blow off, and blow out. They express all sorts of "helpful" suggestions to you, the sibling who lives in the same town with Mom, and then they catch the next stagecoach out of Dodge. When they're in town, Mom's center stage. She's on an energy high. She's dressed in her best and looks great. You, the suffering saint who lives down the street, may be thinking, "This isn't the mom I deal with every day!"

If you are the out-of-town sibling, remember that Mom may be putting on a show just for you. Whether you realize it or not, being with the family for a day is much different than being with them every day. When you come, they are in vacation mode. Mom has put her issues on hold until you leave.

Out-of-town siblings should regularly express their gratitude to those who care for their parents day-to-day. Maybe a note that says, "Thanks, I appreciate all you're doing for the folks—I know it isn't easy." Maybe some unexpected flowers delivered to their door. Maybe an offer to give respite by coming to town for a few days so they can get away. Whatever the form of expressed gratitude, it's important that you acknowledge they are shouldering a heavy load and that you do appreciate their efforts.

> *"My sister lives a mile from our parents and has had to shoulder much of the day-to-day challenges. After my recent weeklong visit home, I realized how much she does and that I need to work harder to find ways to be helpful from a distance."*

Family dynamics play critical roles when the time comes to help parents grow older. Identify your family dynamics and learn to work with them. Understand these relationships are there, they have been the way they are for a long time, and you must accept them. Try not to take things personally, just take them for what they are. Family history helps explain the present, and it helps gauge expectations going forward.

———

*Think about how roles and relationships play out in your family. Where do you fit?*

———

# 5

# CARING CONVERSATIONS

Generally, regardless of our age, we desire to please our parents. We want to do the right things for them "when the time comes." To do the right things as we (and they) grow older, we need to exchange information with them. Wouldn't it be helpful if your parents authored a definitive reference manual entitled, *What to Do If I Get Daffy, Difficult, or Die,* and handed it to you in Act 3 of your family play? Yes, that would be nice.

Some information to be shared is very practical and factual: Where do your parents do their banking? Who is their broker, lawyer, doctor? Do they have a will? A burial plot?

> *"The conversations didn't come easy. I thought it was Mom's reluctance until I realized it was mine."*

Where do they keep the key to their safe deposit box?

Other information is quite personal and emotional: What would Mom like her family to do should she develop a dementia? When the time comes, what kind of funeral arrangements would Dad like?

In addition to information you would like from your parents, there are facts and feelings you want to share with them. A practical fact could be, "Here's how you can reach me when I'm traveling on business." The personal (feeling) might be, "How will I ever repay you for all the grief I caused you during my college years."

In the absence of the "*What to Do If ...*" reference manual, you have conversations with your parents. You ask, listen, talk. These conversations become the foundation and the culmination of your remaining time with your parents, and they go something like this:

"Mom, Dad, there are things you need to tell me, things I need to know." Or, "Mom, Dad, there are things I need to tell you, things I need you to know."

We call the talks caring conversations. In them, facts and feelings are exchanged, parent to child and child to parent. Caring conversations help remove the guesswork surrounding what you and your parents need, think, and feel, and they give direction to meeting their needs.

Over a lifetime, we all find ourselves failing to have important conversations with those we care most about. We don't say what needs to be said. We don't talk about what we feel in our hearts. We often can't find words or muster the courage to express these thoughts. Maybe we feel these talks invade our parents' privacy or acknowledge their mortality. What we've seen is that caring conversations often and easily occur within the context of naturally occurring opportunities. You must be awake to the moment.

A naturally occurring opportunity might follow a parent's visiting a friend in the hospital, as Sharon discovered in the following situation:

> *After seeing her best friend of forty years in a hospital bed after a debilitating stroke, awaiting transfer to the nursing home, Sharon's mother said: "Boy, I sure wouldn't want to live like that." Sharon seized the moment. "Really? Let's talk about that. What would you want to have done?"*

Another naturally occurring opportunity might come when a parent voices concerns about a friend's health. Martin tells of beginning a caring conversation with his father after hearing him comment about his golf partner Lawrence:

> *Martin's dad expressed concern for Lawrence. "He drives like crazy, some days he smells, and some days he totally forgets our tee time. His kids should do something; they should show more interest." It was a perfect opening for Martin, "Dad, what would you want us kids to do if those times ever come with you?"*

When your parents' health dictates they should no longer live at home is always a difficult conversation. If your parents' friends deal with such a situation, it's a perfect, naturally occurring opportunity to discuss the topic. In the following story, an adult child tells about a caring conversation that he and his brother had with their parents after seeing friends undergo a stressful situation:

> *Clarence and Lucille were our parents' best friends. Lucille had debilitating health issues that kept her in a wheelchair. Clarence, a gentle, nurturing soul, cared for Lucille twenty-four/ seven for many years. His devotion took its toll. When their only child, Nancy, pushed for putting Lucille in a nursing home, Clarence became angry with her and felt devastated. In all the years, they had never talked about what would happen "if." When my brother and I talked with our parents about Clarence and Lucille's situation, we talked about their "what if." We had a caring conversation.*

Some talk and topics seem safer while washing dishes after a family dinner, or sharing a coffee, or tending the chores. Adult children often have meaningful conversations with their parents while riding in the car—especially at night. Maybe it's the soothing hum of the engine. Maybe it's that people keep their eyes on the road, thus avoiding eye contact. Maybe it's the comforting blanket of darkness. Or maybe it's that while driving you keep moving ahead and things are left behind. Whatever the reason, people do seem to open up. Know that timing is everything and seize the moment.

The following story tells how Andy began a caring conversation with his mother, Marge, on the ride home from a family member's funeral:

*Marge and Andy drove the forty miles home after Uncle Norbert's funeral. Norbert was Marge's youngest brother and her last living sibling. Norbert had two sons, one daughter, and six grandchildren. His wife, Grace, died several years ago.*

*The funeral was pretty traditional, with a visitation the night before, an open casket in the narthex, and a little lunch in the church basement afterwards. As they drove home, Andy asked his mother, "So, what did you think of the service?" First Marge was tentative, but with some encouragement, a few miles behind them, and some open-ended questions, she began to talk. Before long she detailed things she would like for her service. She suggested some readings and songs, a few remarks from the grandchildren, and the spirit—a spirit of celebration.*

*Andy didn't make any judgments, didn't offer any commentary. Rather, he listened and made mental notes. He used this shared experience, his uncle Norbert's funeral, to grow his understanding of what would please his mother, what she would want when the time came.*

*Andy did ask his mother if she thought they should write this information down for future reference, and she replied without hesitation, "Well, I suppose so, but I'm not going yet!" She promised*

*Andy she would tell him if she changed her mind
on the hymns to sing. Deal.*

*What a pleasant, memorable ride home.*

As you have a caring conversation, keep in mind that parents never stop being parents. Though circumstances may have changed and roles may have reversed, you are still the child. Do your best to let Mom and Dad parent you. It's what you will someday want, too. Together, with mutual respect, you and your parents chart their course with as much clarity as can be foreseen.

Don't underestimate the power of a simple thank you. On Veteran's Day, Gilbert tells his octogenarian father, "Thanks, Dad, for the time you served in World War II. I know you sacrificed a lot, and I've always appreciated it." Like most of those crusty war veterans, Gilbert's dad says little and just shrugs his shoulders in that "Oh it was nothing" way. He's from a generation that doesn't express feelings as well as Gilbert's, but that doesn't mean his emotions don't run as deep.

> *"I could never express my love for Mom and Dad in my own words, so I let Hallmark say it for me. After Mom died, I found a box containing nearly every card I sent her. I was glad they meant a lot to her."*

Many wait too long to have caring conversations with their parents. It's almost a guarantee that, if you do, the outcome will be less than optimal. Anticipate. Communicate.

Act 3 can also be a perfect time to bury old hatchets. Doing so will usually occur in a caring conversation that begins,

"You know, Dad, I've always wanted to tell you how sorry I was for ..." Or, "Mom, I've never been able to say this until now, but did you know ..."

Here's an example of a family who sadly couldn't find a way to bury the hatchet:

> *Donald and Doris were a wonderful couple, well into their eighties, who had one child, Bill. For reasons unknown to anyone outside these three, the parents and son had not spoken or seen each other for three decades. Donald was eventually transferred to a local nursing home, and when Doris died, Bill came to see his dad. The trust officer asked Donald if he could take Bill to visit his parents' house so he could see where his parents had spent the past thirty years. Donald gave his approval. As the son and trust officer entered the house, the son immediately saw numerous childhood pictures of himself on the shelves and walls. The trust officer said, "You were always a big part of their lives." Overwhelmed, Bill wept.*

I have been present at many hospital and hospice settings where a parent's death is imminent. Family has gathered, the parent is unresponsive, there's a wringing of hands, and a fog of finality hangs over the scene—

> *"I took comfort in the hospice nurse telling me that hearing was the last sense to be lost in dying. I spoke the words I needed to say, but I wish I had said them earlier to hear her response."*

regardless of the relationships the adult children and parent have had. The end is near.

People of science have proven that hearing is the last of the senses to go, so loved ones are encouraged to *say* whatever final words they want to say, even if their parent can't respond. The words will be heard. I have served as hall monitor in these types of settings, signaling adult children from the waiting room when it's their turn to have their last moments with their parent. Whether two minutes or twenty are spent, great comfort comes from this final time together.

As I'm with families in these deathbed settings, I hope that the adult children haven't saved things they wished they had said sooner. For a satisfying close to Act 3, adult children need to have shared their sentiments while their parents could respond. How sad the adult child who delivers a monologue rather than having a dialogue with his or her parent. How sweeter to say it sooner and relish—or be affirmed by—the response. The forgiveness, the affirmation, the "Me too, son." That's powerful.

The story that follows tells of Brad's poignant visit with his dying mother. It illustrates the way in which many adult children would like to say goodbye to a beloved parent.

> *Brad's seventy-year-old mother lay dying of cancer. Throughout their lives he and she were as close as a mother and son could be. Her dying provided another opportunity for a caring conversation. Brad agonized over how to initiate his final goodbye. Too soon and his mom might lose her will to live; too late and he'd never get*

*the chance. He chose a Friday night to be alone with her. Nurses placed a handwritten Do Not Disturb sign on the closed, hospital room door.*

*Brad had written her eulogy and held it in his trembling hands. He said, "Mom, I've written something that will be shared at your memorial service. I'd like to read it to you."*

*"That would be nice," she replied, and added quietly, "I'll just lie here and close my eyes."*

*Several minutes and two pages later, Brad spoke the last line, then collapsed into his mom's arms. They sobbed for nearly as long as the reading took. Then they dried their eyes and talked for an hour. Just the two of them, looking intently at each other and saying how much they loved one another, how great their lives had been, and how they would do it all again, exactly the same way if given the chance. They knew that not all of their time together was perfect, but there was no "I wish we had done ..." or "I'm sorry I did ..." They paused at times and Brad's mom rested, her eyes closed. After one bit of silence she opened them and said weakly, "You're so nice." She died peacefully a few days later.*

If you're lucky, you will have an opportunity to say goodbye to your parent as Brad did. It may be your most mean-

ingful caring conversation. It will be your last. Don't save it
for the eulogy.

---

***Start two lists:***
***1. What you need to know.***
***2. What you need to say.***

---

# 6

# No One Can Do Everything; Everyone Can Do Something

Let's begin with a story about Aileen that shows how helpful it is to have a sibling orchestrate the help of family members when a crisis occurs:

> *Aileen e-mailed and phoned her four siblings and their spouses regularly. She provided the glue that kept them informed about their parent-related goings-on. A medical crisis came out of the blue; Dad needed hospitalization and surgery. Aileen took charge, and with her guidance, the family rose to the occasion. The gals seemed to mobilize best. They figured out what needed to be done and made sure it happened. But the guys stepped up to the plate, too. Aileen saw that some family mem-*

*bers immediately rolled up their sleeves and asked
how they could help. Others sat back and waited
to be asked. She realized she couldn't make any
assumptions about who was doing what. Instead, she made sure to give explicit assignments
and await confirmation that the assignments
had been accepted. Dad recovered just fine, and
everyone in the family felt good about their con-
tributions to his getting back on track.*

In this story, Aileen mobilizes her family to respond to
a crisis, and, thankfully, all goes well. Many of your parents'
growing-older needs in Act 3 won't be crisis-related, but they
still must be addressed. Anticipate, communicate, delegate,
and prepare. That's what you need to do. But anticipate what?
And delegate what?

We've created a list of most
common needs for you. From our
experience, these are the main
parent-growing-older needs your
family should anticipate, discuss,
and then delegate to family members. The list is not definitive; it's

> *"Mom had a tendency
> to rag on Dad and
> complain about him, but
> we girls all saw how
> much he did for her."*

a start. Your list will reflect circumstances unique to your
family. You can and should change your list week-to-week,
month-to-month—whenever you see a change in need or a
change in who has agreed to respond to the need.

## List of Most Common Needs
- Finances
- Healthcare decisions
- Home maintenance
- Errands
- Weekly chores
- Personal care
- Transportation
- First responder
- Communications
- Technologist
- Researcher

You will be a step ahead of most families if you discuss these needs with your family and assign roles to family members before parent-related crises occur. This can be a fun family project that keeps everyone involved. Your family members become a team with a common goal of seeing that your parents have the love and support they need. The key step is ensuring that each family member knows and accepts his or her role in achieving the goal.

Calling a family meeting, electronically or in person, is a good way to begin the dialogue around the question "Who can help with what?" Start with the assumption that everyone can do something. The assignments can be tricky. Often the family member who lives closest or has the best rapport with Mom or Dad gets stuck with more than his or her fair share of work. Or maybe the lion's share of work falls on the oldest child's plate. Make sure the assignments are distributed as evenly and as fairly as possible. Keep in mind, too, that you can ask people outside the family to fulfill certain needs.

Through the entire exercise, know that everybody can do something. When you complete your discussions, record your assignments in a table as shown:

## SAMPLE
*Most Common Needs Assignments Table*
*Date: February 21, 2009*

|  | Finances | Healthcare Decisions | Home Maintenance | Errands | Weekly Chores | Personal Care | Transportation | First Responder | Communications | Technologist | Researcher |
|---|---|---|---|---|---|---|---|---|---|---|---|
| Bob |  | √ |  |  |  |  |  |  |  |  |  |
| Mary |  |  | √ | √ |  |  |  |  |  |  |  |
| Sybil |  |  |  |  |  |  |  |  | √ |  |  |
| Betty |  |  |  |  |  | √ |  |  |  |  |  |
| Gary | √ |  |  |  |  |  |  |  |  |  | √ |
| Sue |  |  |  |  | √ |  |  |  |  |  |  |
| Larry |  |  |  | √ |  |  |  |  |  |  |  |
| Helen |  |  |  |  |  |  |  | √ |  |  |  |
| Adam |  |  |  |  |  |  |  |  |  | √ |  |
| Jessica |  |  |  |  |  | √ |  |  |  |  |  |

While you're working with your family to assign responsibilities, create a contact list using a form like the one that follows with one row per contact. Share a copy with all who are on the list. This information fosters effective and more frequent communication among family members, and it's invaluable in times of crisis.

## Contact Information

| Name | Relationship to Parents | Contact Information |
|------|------------------------|---------------------|
|      |                        |                     |
|      |                        | Daytime phone |
|      |                        | Evening phone |
|      |                        | Cell phone |
|      |                        | E-mail address |
|      |                        | Mailing address |
|      |                        | Daytime phone |
|      |                        | Evening phone |
|      |                        | Cell phone |
|      |                        | E-mail address |
|      |                        | Mailing address |

## Most Common Needs

*Finances*

Money matters are fairly universal. Whether your parents are wealthy or constantly stretch to make ends meet, someone will probably have to help manage their financial affairs at some point. Many older adults view managing their money as an acid test of their independence, so tread carefully. Assign a family member to this need who not only has financial skills, but who can have caring conversations about the topic with your parents. The person assigned should be creative in his or her approach to minimize damage to funds or feelings.

Money matters include asset management, tax obligations, monthly bill paying, insurance, Medicare submissions and reconciliations, pension benefits, veterans' benefits, and paperwork associated with public assistance eligibility and recertification. The person assigned the financial responsibility should watch the weekly flow of mail to the parents' home. Wading through the volumes of mail can be time-consuming, confusing, and frustrating. Realize that the financial role can be a full-time job.

> *"It's not that the guys didn't care; they simply didn't know what to do. They just needed direction. They felt good about helping the folks."*

Depending on your parents' financial circumstances and whether they have prepared a power of attorney document, you may want the services of an attorney to help get things in order. For some families, the services of a professional trust officer can also be helpful, especially if there are substantial or complicated assets, a lack of trust among family members, a reluctance on the part of your parent to relinquish control to a child, or, simply, the lack of time or talent among the family members. Hiring a professional in this area is often money well spent.

Consider this: If your parents have not made arrangements, encourage them to select the person they want to manage their finances while they are able to make that determination rather than waiting until someone, perhaps the courts, will appoint someone for them. If your parent is hospitalized, you might consider enlisting the help of the hospital social worker who can ask this as a "routine" question. The hospital will have the necessary forms and notary publics, and the social worker can assist with completing the document.

The financial power of attorney does not need to live close to the parent. The family member assigned might consider making use of the auto-pay feature for monthly bills. The family member might also consider setting up charge accounts wherever he or she can and have the business bill them monthly. This is a handy way of seeing how your parents spend their money. Also, he or she should be attentive to any e-mail access your parents may have to accounts and put in place the necessary controls.

Finally, keep in mind that the power of attorney authority ends the moment the parent dies. From then on, the person the parent has designated to be the executor has control of financial matters.

*Healthcare Decisions*

Assign someone in your family to help determine your parents' healthcare wishes. Encourage your parents to designate someone as their healthcare agent while they are still able to choose. The family member designated as the healthcare agent will be expected to speak for the family when interacting with your parents' healthcare providers.

The family member assigned this role should ask questions of your parents related to life supports, extraordinary interventions, palliative care, and nursing home placement. They should discuss some what-if scenarios and have your parents tell them what they would want the family to do in various situations. Answers to these questions come through caring conversations, and they remove the guesswork from what to do at times of crisis. Your family needs to know your parents' healthcare wishes should the occasion arise where they can't speak on their own behalf. You want your parents to be in ultimate control of their destiny. This helps remove the finger of blame and the feeling of guilt.

> *"Let your parent have input as to the decisions concerning their care and living arrangements. Listen to them."*

The family member serving as the healthcare agent should share the parents' wishes with the rest of the family so they have an idea what will happen when the time comes.

If your parent enters a hospital without having the advance healthcare directive document in place, ask the social worker to assist. If your parent is seeing an attorney about estate planning, ask the attorney to address this issue as well.

Your parents will find comfort in getting their documents in order.

As with the financial power of attorney, the family member your parent assigns as their healthcare agent does not need to live close to your parents. They simply need to be available to take phone calls from healthcare providers and make the necessary decisions for your parent's care.

### Home Maintenance

Issues of home maintenance will persist as long as your parents live in their own home. Sometimes the sons, sons-in-law, nieces, nephews, and grandchildren will enjoy helping with these tasks. The family members assigned to meeting this need should feel comfortable taking direction from the parents and be capable of managing the tasks in a way that pleases them. They may have to follow instructions that don't make a lot of sense. For example, Mom wants snow removed from her driveway before she leaves the garage. She does not want tire tracks in the snow left on the driveway. Whoever is shoveling needs to know that it needs to be done before nine o'clock or she will be out there doing it herself. Those assigned home maintenance tasks should live close by, but major home projects may involve many family members who gather from various and far-away locations to paint the house, for example, or build a new deck.

### Errands

The person assisting with errands should live relatively close to the parents. Most important, this person needs the patience of Job. Parents sometimes insist on making several trips to a store before they deem an item—a sweater, for example—suitable for purchase. Even when they buy an item in a single trip, they can take forever to do so. Older people like purchasing the same brand of item, but brands and packaging change and this may frustrate them (and the person helping them!). Find a family member who enjoys shopping and can make the activity fun for the parent. Not everyone has these skills.

An adult child tells how his mother made a sport of running errands:

> *Each morning, Mother penned her to-do list and made sure by day's end that she had checked off all items on it. Managing this list kept her engaged, industrious, and in control. I thought some items were unnecessary, some silly, and most were random rather than grouped for efficiency, but I decided to keep my opinions to myself.*

The person assigned this task should consider catalog shopping as an option. Also, they should develop a list of stores that deliver. Many communities now have online ordering services and will deliver groceries and sundries for a small fee.

### Weekly Chores

At some point in their lives, your parents will need and appreciate help with chores such as doing laundry, changing bedding, vacuuming and dusting, mowing the lawn, and preparing meals. Family members who live close by may be assigned some of these tasks, but your family may also arrange for the services of a housekeeper. Finding the right one is key. Ideally, the housekeeper will develop a lasting friendship with your parents and provide a frequent and fun social contact.

> *"We found that talking to each other was healthy for our family. Once we decided to be open and caring with one another, we were able to move on and focus on Dad's needs."*

Meals, because your parents need them three times each day, pose a more challenging problem than housekeeping. In some families, members take turns providing meals. They make enough meals for an entire week and put them in their parents' freezer. Then Mom and Dad can microwave the meals as needed. Access to predictable nutritious meals should not be a barrier. All communities have congregate dining and home-delivered meals options. Also, many local restaurants deliver meals from their menus.

Whoever helps with chores needs to be mindful that older persons may see others helping them as an invasion of privacy or a loss of independence. Your parents may see others helping them as a sign that they are losing their independence. They may view help as an invasion of their privacy. If this happens, step back, re-evaluate, and proceed with caution.

### Personal Care

Parents living at home reach a point in their lives when they need help with personal care activities such as bathing, shaving, cutting their toenails, getting dressed, and going to the bathroom. Ordering their medication refills and setting up their medications are tasks not quite as personal, but they are still important and fall into this need category. A family member with nursing skills who lives near the parents may be best for the role.

When this need rises in priority—especially when a parent's incontinence becomes a problem, it's wise that your family begins researching in-home healthcare, assisted living, and nursing home options. Our experience proves that families should start educating themselves at that point in time if not before, so they are prepared for making informed decisions about their parents' care.

### Transportation

Your parent likely needs transportation to places such as the beauty shop, barber, church, grocery store, and library. This assignment can be ideal for a family member who wants to do something but doesn't want—or can't handle—too much responsibility. They must be dependable and willing and able to help your parent in and out of the car. This job could be perfect for the teenage driver who might be the beneficiary of Grandfather's car.

Sometimes neighbors and friends can take your parents to church. They are going anyway and don't mind stopping by for your parents. They will be less likely to take them to and from appointments. Sometimes a sister or sister-in-law of your parent might be willing to take on this responsibility. She might even plan a lunch outing with the appointment.

### First Responder

The first responder should be someone who lives near your parents who can be first on the scene if an emergency should arise. Family members, friends, or neighbors can be assigned this role. First responders need to determine who to contact in a crisis. They need to make good decisions under stress, remain calm, and buoy the spirits of other family members. If not a family member, the first responder should be told what the boundaries are. Once the situation is handled and the responsible party of record is notified, the first responder has completed his or her role. It may not be necessary or appropriate to include them in an ongoing family medical situation.

### Communications

Keeping everyone informed is key throughout your Act 3. Have one person take charge of family communications. He or she can create a master list of e-mail addresses, telephone numbers, and mailing addresses. This communicator may broadcast important messages to all family members, making sure that everyone receives new information at the same time. This person needs not live close to your parents. The family communicator may also initiate family gatherings and remind all of birthdays, anniversaries, and family events.

### Technologist

Many older people love e-mailing and surfing the net. You should assign a technology-savvy family member to act as personal help desk so your parents know whom to call when things don't work as planned. With today's technologies, the family member can be miles away and remotely access and fix your parents' computer. This person could also help with seemingly minor adjustments that make a big difference to them—for example, showing your parents how to increase the size of the objects on their computer screen, or type documents in large font sizes, or set up address lists for groups of people they e-mail frequently. Private family websites can be set up and accessed by password where family members share news and photos. This is the job for that teenage technology guru. If you need to seek computer help outside your family, try to find someone in the community that can stop by your parents' home. Tech support is much easier in person than over the phone.

### Researcher

Every family needs a researcher, a person with an insatiable appetite for information, who searches the Internet for answers to questions not readily available elsewhere. Find the member of your family who can navigate the world of Google. This family member can be turned loose to help investigate and recommend things such as possible retirement communities, assisted living centers, or nursing homes for your parents. If your parent has been diagnosed with a certain disease, the researcher can help find out all that's been written about it. This person need not live near your parents. He or she simply needs to agree to share his or her findings with your family so that it can be used to help you make informed decisions.

There you have the Most Common Needs in a nutshell. Take comfort in knowing the categories of needs that will arise in your Act 3. Take heed to assign your family members to them. Use this as a chance to enhance family communication and rapport. Remember, everyone can do something.

The following story, told by the adult son of a widower, illustrates how his sister Margaret helped distribute work among family members that had fallen on the shoulders of Linda, the adult son's wife.

*My dad was always partial to my wife, Linda. After Mother died, Linda and Dad became particularly close. Linda called or visited Dad daily. She planned his menus, shopped for his groceries, and kept his house clean and functioning.*

*As time passed, Linda became even more involved in Dad's life. She took him to medical appointments, balanced his checkbook, and waded through the monthly mailings from Medicare. As Dad's functional and cognitive abilities failed, he became more dependent on Linda, and she spent more time helping him. I appreciated what Linda was doing, but I had no idea the extent.*

*When Linda and I took a week's vacation to see the kids in Ohio, my sister Margaret came from Kansas to be with Dad. When we returned, she was in a state of mild outrage.*

*"I'm exhausted! I had no idea! Daddy is so needy and so dependent on Linda. He's very time-consuming and, no surprise, he's pretty demanding.*

*I don't know how Linda has done it all this time.
We need to pitch in and help."*

*Margaret was right. Dad's need for support, as-
sistance, and companionship had grown signifi-
cantly since Mother's death. Linda was doing it
all.*

*As was her style, Margaret took charge and via e-
mail invitation convened a family meeting. My
two brothers and their wives and two of the older
grandchildren were included. Before we knew it,
Margaret and Linda had charted Dad's needs to
live independently and had assigned each of us
roles and tasks to play and perform in support of
his needs. All the bases were covered, and no one,
including the grandchildren and Steve and Ann
in Alaska, left without something to do.*

*Margaret made the point: No one can do every-
thing. Everyone can do something.*

What if you are an only child? The insights we've shared
in this chapter still apply to you and your parents. You don't
have siblings to work with as a team to see that your parents
have the support they need. The positive in this situation is
that there won't be sibling disagreements about parent care.
Also, there's no possibility that you will be dealing with a
do-nothing brother or sister. Because of this, your role can
be less stressful, though not necessarily less work, than if

you were in a multi-sibling family. In many cases, we've seen that the only adult child's spouse takes more responsibility than he or she would have if siblings were involved. Also, if you have children, they can help their grandfather or grandmother in many ways, creating memorable intergenerational experiences. Therefore, if you are an only child, it's still true that the "everyone" you enlist can do something, and keep in mind that you don't have to do it all.

---

*Jot down who you know who could help with what when the time comes.*

---

# 7

# Navigating the Big Ds: Dementia, Drinking, Depression, and Driving

As we go through life with our parents, we are mostly unaware that they are growing older until one day in our Act 3 something happens: they miss paying a bill, they leave a kettle on the burner or a burned pan in the oven, they cause a minor fender bender. Suddenly, we realize our parents might be showing signs of aging. Sometimes the signs mean nothing. Everyone has occasionally missed a payment or forgotten a bubbling kettle when they simply had too much on their mind. At other times, though, the signs are early indicators of things to come.

We refer to some of these more serious things to come as the Big Ds: dementia, drinking, depression, and driving.

We'll share some of our experiences and thoughts about each.

## Dementia

We all feel we're losing it at times. We even joke we have "some timers" when we forget or misplace things. Older adults are often supersensitive to signs they might be getting Alzheimer's (a form of dementia). One man was so bothered by the idea of Alzheimer's he invented a new condition he called "information constipation." When family members begin to see signs, they fear the worst. Admittedly, dementia is frightening, but we have watched families manage it extremely well. The keys to accepting or navigating this new reality in your life involves adjusting your expectations of what your parent can or can't do accordingly, not arguing with your parent (if they think every day is Thursday, then, okay, it's Thursday) and knowing where to turn for professional help.

> *"As Mother's dementia advanced, she actually became sweeter and more loving. What a special privilege to witness her graceful life closure."*

The first thing we suggest to adult children who fear their parent is in the early stages of dementia is to have the parent see his or her doctor, who should treat the matter seriously. We remind them that nearly 80 percent of people over eighty-five *don't* have dementia, so the disease is often misdiagnosed. Overmedication, dehydration, infections, and depression can all look like dementia in an older person. What may appear to be an untreatable disease may be very treatable. Get thee to a doctor!

If your parent refuses to cooperate, do your best to determine why the reluctance and then work with what you know. You might call your parent's doctor, explain the situation, and ask for help. The doctor could call your parent with an "it's time to come in for a routine physical" call. If your parent won't follow your advice to seek help, who might he or she listen to? Have that person offer the suggestion for them to see their doctor.

If your parent does see a doctor and receives a diagnosis of a kind of dementia, you then have a framework in which to work. You can begin the process of education. Be prepared for it to be harder on you than it will be on your parent. Memory loss is associated with many forms of dementia and it's a paradox. One of the greatest sadnesses of dementia is the loss of memory. One of the greatest blessings of this disease is the loss of memory. The older person with dementia cannot process and remember all that the diagnosis will mean for him or her. This is a blessing. Don't spend much time on the diagnosis; rather begin to accept the situation. Learn about it so you can live with it.

Things won't change dramatically overnight. You will still have many joyous times together as you navigate this journey. As the following story illustrates, there will no doubt come the time when your parent will have spent a wonderful day and not recall it the next day. Take comfort in knowing that he or she had a wonderful time at the time.

*Joe's wife, Clara, had Alzheimer's. Joe, a devoted husband, dutifully took Clara for a ride in the country. Every afternoon they traveled the exact same route. Clara loved it. Every day she rode in a brand new car, saw sights she had never seen before, and spent time with the man she dearly loved. Joe concluded, "It didn't really matter what kind of dementia my wife had. In her reality, she had a wonderful life every day of those last years."*

Photos can be helpful in reminding the person of the memories. This then can be the basis of another meaningful day spent together reminiscing. Photos often remind them of things from their youth. They more easily remember events of years ago than events from the day before, which can provide you an opportunity to hear more of their life stories.

Usually, people with dementia are quite content with their new reality; if so, don't fight it. Take your cues from them and try not to impose your standards, because they likely won't be able to meet them. If, for example, your mom wants to wear the same dress every day, buy five of them so there is a clean one for each day. If something must be done, find a way to accomplish it with the least disruption to your parent. The following story illustrates how adult children's good intentions may not have the results they intend:

*Jane's daughters noticed that her clothes were ragged. Out of love for their mom, the daughters decided that while she was away for a short time, they would clean her closet and replace her ragged clothes with some nice new ones. Their good intentions backfired. Jane was horrified when she*

*saw "someone else's" clothes in her closet. She com-*
*plained, "Those are not my clothes. I have never*
*worn other people's clothes, and I won't start now!*
*Where are my clothes?" Jane's daughters brought*
*back their mother's ragged wardrobe. They might*
*have succeeded had they replaced one old outfit at*
*a time.*

Dementia introduces situations in your family's life that you won't like, can't control, and don't understand. To cope, your family will need to modify their perceptions and expectations. Along the way you will have chances to be creative, as Virginia is in the following situation:

*Virginia's aunt Gladys awoke in the middle of*
*nearly every night, put on her shoes, and wan-*
*dered about the neighborhood. One evening after*
*Gladys went to bed, Virginia hid her shoes in the*
*closet. Gladys would never think of going outside*
*barefoot, so when she awoke and couldn't find her*
*shoes, she simply went back to bed, never to wan-*
*der again.*

Gone are the days when adult services professionals tried to bring the cognitively impaired person back to reality with painful truths. If a person commented that their mother had visited them the previous evening, the old school approach was to confront them with the harsh

> *"As sad as it is, we find the humor and keep perspective. Dad would want it that way."*

fact that she had been dead for several years. This inevitably caused a great deal of sadness and anxiety for the person. "You mean my mother died, and I missed the funeral?"

Healthcare professionals now realize the individuals' contentment is more important than knowing the truth, even if it means playing along with them. Sometimes they employ a bit of good-intentioned acting, too, as they did with Bob.

> *Bob was a cantankerous old guy in the nursing home. He had many delusions, but one day he wanted to go for a swim in the community indoor pool. He would not accept the fact that he wasn't able to swim and couldn't go. In desperation, the staff solicited help from the nursing home administrator and asked if he could take a call from Bob regarding the status of the pool. The administrator assumed the role of the pool manager and simply told Bob that he was terribly sorry, the pool was down for maintenance that day and he wouldn't be able to swim. Bob accepted the news. Someone had finally told him the "truth."*

Sometimes families become overwhelmed with the day-to-day management of dementia. Educate yourself on the disease and approaches to dealing with it so you can gauge expectations. Your parent's doctor can be an excellent resource. He or she will prescribe pharmaceutical interventions if available and will share information regarding possible side effects.

The Alzheimer's Association is another excellent resource. They can provide you with reading materials regarding the disease, its likely progression, and its treatment. Most communities have caregiver support groups that will give fresh perspectives on what others are doing to cope. This is a great time to do a family inventory and enlist everyone's help in caring for the individual. Writing letters, sending newsy e-mails, and sharing photographs of grandchildren, nieces, and nephews can provide hours of entertainment for your parent. They read the same letter over and over and over thinking each reading is their first. For this reason, cards and letters are often times more meaningful than phone calls.

Caregiving is hard work. Take care of yourself. If you need a break, explore respite care for your parent with a local long-term-care or assisted-living facility. A temporary stay can help lay the groundwork for an eventual placement if care needs exceed what your family can provide.

It is sad, but the journey can be delightful if you keep your sense of humor and accept your parent's reality with each new day.

### Drinking

Be honest. What role has drinking played in your family? Has alcoholism been present or prevalent? Do your parents have an occasional social drink and a nightly highball? What is normal for them? Any signs of their moving away from normal—in frequency of drinking or amount of drinking—should send danger signals. Also, what they tell you about their drinking

> *"Brother James paid Mother's bills. We became concerned when he noticed Mother's monthly liquor bill doubled."*

may not be true. When you visit them, check the number of alcohol bottles or cans of beer in their refrigerator, liquor cabinet, and pantry. Informally monitor how much your parents are drinking. Red flags arise when you see your parents seeking out opportunities to drink or drinking alone.

As with any change you spot in your parent's routine, seek first to understand. If Mom's been a teetotaler her entire life and now can't seem to do without a drink or two each day, ask her why she's begun. You might discover she has been having a hard time sleeping at night and the alcohol helps her nod off more quickly. If so, a moderate amount of alcohol should not be a problem. One thing to check, though, would be her medications and the stipulation regarding use of alcohol with them.

After you determine what's behind her drinking, you might suggest other solutions. For example, if sleeplessness is the problem, some light exercise during the day might help Mom relax and rest more soundly.

Here's a good example of why it's important to seek first to understand:

> *Several proper church ladies put up a fuss when their pastor changed the time of their Sunday service. They raised a major ruckus, but it was never clear to the pastor why they were concerned. After some probing, he learned the ladies were upset because for years their routine had been to attend church, return to their apartments for a drink or two, and then dine at a Sunday brunch. The Sunday service time change cut short their time*

*for a cocktail. They didn't have a drinking problem; they just didn't like their routine disrupted.*

If alcohol has become a problem, the family will need to take some action. The problem is not likely to solve itself, and the sooner you begin interventions the better for everyone. The skills and comfort level of your family members as well as all their personality traits and communication styles will determine the interventions you will be willing to try.

Some parents will listen to their children's concerns and change their consumption levels. Others will deny they have a problem and will refuse to listen to any sort of intervention. In this case, you should involve their doctor, and if the problem persists, your parent may be placed in an in-patient treatment setting. If the problem continues, your parent may be told they can no longer live independently. In all cases, the earlier the intervention, the more positive the outcome for all.

## Depression

One definition of depression talks about it being a response to real or imagined loss. Any wonder, then, that depression is common among older people considering the losses they experience? How would any of us feel about losing our independence, experiencing loss of control over our lives and loss of any of our five senses, decision-making abilities, status in life,

> *"I wish I had known more about depression in the elderly—how to recognize it and where to get help."*

or spouse and friends? Add to the mix side effects of medications, and we would not feel good. We might well feel depressed. Growing older is not for the faint of heart.

What distinguishes clinical depression from a general sadness, the blues, or just being down? Signs of depression vary from person to person. Some simply lose their interest in the world around them and are unwilling to participate in activities with family and friends. Mom no longer goes to the beauty shop. Dad no longer meets the guys for breakfast on Wednesdays. They go to bed earlier and get up later. Perhaps they stay in their bedclothes for the entire day. Sometimes a parent will stop eating and experience a weight loss, or sometimes they will overeat and gain weight. Some will be unable to fall asleep or stay asleep. Others will cry easily or become easily angered. Some will increase their alcohol consumption. In most cases, one symptom will lead to another and another. On top of it all, your parent may become confused as to time and events. Occasionally, a person will talk about "wishing it was over" or "ending it all." If you hear this, seek professional help. The sooner depression is named and treated, the higher the chances for its effective management.

Many older adults are uncomfortable with the notion of being depressed. They are from a generation that didn't address mental health issues, often believing that depression would be viewed as a weakness or defect. They might say, "I'm not depressed," or "I just need to toughen up." Some adult children have success talking to their parent this way: "I've noticed you seem quieter than usual and don't seem to be sleeping well. I'm wondering if we should mention this to your doctor during our next visit."

If you sense Mom won't be receptive to even mentioning the subject during her next checkup, speak privately with her doctor. Explain what you are seeing and why you feel your mom might be depressed. Let the doctor know that your mom will be reluctant to acknowledge depression. Suggest that the doctor explain the problem using the symptoms rather than the diagnosis of depression. He may be able to prescribe something for your mom that will relieve the presenting symptoms. After all, if she is depressed, she is in fact not feeling very well emotionally.

Here's how Hazel convinced her husband, Ralph, that an antidepressant would be good for him:

> *Hazel and Ralph shared small living quarters in an assisted-living center. Ralph had always been short tempered, but as time passed, he became nearly impossible to live with. Hazel discussed the situation with the nurse and asked if she could prescribe something for Ralph that would make him less irritable. The nurse spoke to Ralph's doctor, who agreed to start him on a mild antidepressant. When Ralph asked Hazel why he should take the pill, she said, "It helps you think better." Without any other information, Ralph began taking the medication, and within a few weeks, he had calmed down considerably. Hazel felt better, too.*

If you know of others who are being treated successfully for depression, share this positive news with your parent. Maybe a friend who has struggled with depression is doing better with the help of medication. Perhaps your parent would value the opinion of a minister, social worker, or granddaughter. Don't be afraid to enlist someone's help in addressing this problem.

Your parent's doctor may have some concerns about prescribing medications for depression. As with any medication, there can be side effects such as drowsiness or dizziness that can lead to an increase in falls, and they might interfere with other medications or alcohol. Increasingly doctors are being scrutinized for their use of antipsychotic or mood-altering drugs. Some doctors will only prescribe something if the person agrees he or she is depressed and is willing to take a medication for it. The irony is that depressed people are usually the last to see that they might be depressed.

After your parent starts mood-altering medications, remember that it will take several days or weeks to see the effects. Often your parent will say after a few days that they have stopped taking the medication because it isn't doing any good. Encourage (no, insist) that they continue taking it.

Treating depression can be the best gift you and your parent will ever share. Following treatment, many older adults are once again able to enjoy the company of their family and friends and take part in the activities they had previously enjoyed.

## Driving

Asking your mom or dad to hand the car keys over to you is awkward at best, impossible at worst. Doing so puts you in a "parenting your parent" situation, as Tim discovered in the following story:

*At age sixteen, freedom, power, and independence are spelled c-a-r. Getting a driver's license and having access to a car are the rights of passage, the holy grail of early adolescence.*

*At Tim's house it didn't matter how well he did on the Department of Motor Vehicles written exam or its anxiety-inducing road test. No, at Tim's house, his dad declared him ready to drive.*

*"Son, it would be terrible if you had an accident and hurt someone." So, Dad satisfied himself that Tim's vision, hearing, reflexes, and cognitive abilities were worthy of keys to the 1956 Buick Roadmaster Riviera. At Tim's house, Dad gave the green light to driving.*

*Fast-forward forty years and once again freedom, power, and independence are spelled c-a-r. And, once again, the issues are vision, hearing, reflexes, and cognitive abilities.*

*But wait! Now the roles are reversed. Tim now says, "Dad, it would be terrible if you had an accident and hurt someone."*

*Tim found himself in the contentious position of having to give the driving red light to his dad!*

One morning at the coffee shop, a group of older individuals chatted about driving. A man in his early nineties recalled when he knew it was time for him to slide from behind the wheel. "My wife and I had a cabin in northern Minnesota we loved going to every weekend in the summer. It was a straight four-hour drive there. The problem was, I couldn't drive straight anymore!"

> *"We arranged to have the car taken away from Dad, but unbeknown to us, he ordered another one."*

We wish all older adults would voluntarily stop driving when they should, but they don't, so their children agonize over when and how to convince a parent to hand over the keys.

A conversation that goes as follows can lead to the desired results: "Mom, how would you feel if you caused an accident that seriously hurt you or others? Do you realize how terrible this would be and the family stress it could cause?"

Sometimes a friend of your parent can break the news by saying they no longer feel safe riding with him or her. Some parents will listen to their doctor's advice. A social worker, pastor, or another professional your parent respects as a final authority may be able to convince him or her.

You may have all of these people share their concerns, but the responsibility to take the keys away from Mom or Dad—unpopular with them as it might be—will be up to you to make and communicate. It may help to say, "Mom, Dr. Bowman (doctor), Ann (friend and neighbor), Dick (a cousin), and Howard (the administrator) each have told you it's time you quit driving. They can't ALL be wrong, can they?"

The resolve to keep one's car can be as strong as the will to live, as the staff at a retirement community has seen:

> *A gentleman in a retirement community took pride in the fact that stall #1 in the parking garage was reserved for his car. Though he became a bilateral amputee confined to a wheelchair in his one-bedroom apartment, he refused to sell his car and give up that stall. "By God, that's my car," he said with pride as the car keys dangled from a ring on his belt loop. The maintenance men went out quarterly and pumped air in the tires.*

Some families disconnect the carburetors on their parent's car when they feel the parent shouldn't be driving. They'll say a part is on back order, and, eventually, the parent forgets about driving. One delightfully demented parent, after waiting some time for the part that didn't (and wouldn't) arrive, called her favorite car dealer and said, "Bill, send over another Volvo, would you." One family member called the Department of Motor Vehicles and asked that they test the father-in-law who was coming in that day to renew his license. He failed the parking test three times, so they took away his license. He saved face and never drove again.

Sometimes the forgetfulness associated with aging can work to a family's advantage:

> *Morrie was particularly resistant to giving up the keys to his car even though he had had many close calls with his driving. He had much respect*

*for his doctor, who told him he couldn't drive un-*
*til after the twenty-fourth of the month. For the*
*next six months he told his family that he would*
*be able to drive after the twenty-fourth. Eventu-*
*ally he forgot about driving and the family was*
*able to take the car.*

Retirement centers across the country have dust-caked cars in their parking garages that haven't been licensed or driven for the past five years. Older adults know that they never get back the things they give up as they age, so they hang on to what they can as long as they can. Their reasoning: "This is just one more thing you're telling me I can't do. Well, I think I'll just keep doing it." Driving equates to independence, which people hate to relinquish.

If your parent refuses to hand over the keys, it is possible to negotiate an acceptable alternative. For example, if you can't entirely stop your dad's driving, you might be able to convince him to reduce the frequency. Ask that he stop driving after dark. Some families arrange for a driver for their parents, which allows them to keep their car. Van and bus services reduce the need for personal driving. Some stores deliver merchandise to homes. Taxicabs provide viable options, as do home care agencies. Some parents transition from their car to an electric golf cart. Finally, convincing parents to give or sell their car to a grandchild can also be a way to have them feel good about giving up their car. If it's going to Billy, it will still be in the family.

Be persistent about this issue. You may save one or more lives as a result of what you accomplish.

---

*Stop and think. What signs are you seeing?*

---

# 8

# STUFF MATTERS

Over a lifetime each of us can be defined and understood by our possessions, the stuff we deem valuable: jewelry, clothes, antiques, a fly rod collection, cars, paintings, sculptures, china, or a shop filled with Stanley woodworking tools. They can reveal our hopes and our hobbies, our lifestyles and our values. As time passes, the stuff accumulates—sometimes big time. The point is: stuff matters. It has meaning and consequences.

Though stuff matters, we know that one man's treasure can be another's junk. An adult child tells of her mother's collection that was precious to her, but not so precious to others:

> *My mother collected salt and pepper shakers. It was an obsession, a passion. Whenever we traveled, or when family or friends traveled, the collection grew. Before he died, Dad even remodeled a bedroom in their home to display her prized*

*collection. The Trempealeau County Gazette
once did a feature story on Mom and her nine
hundred sets of shakers. She was so proud. It was
kind of cute. When Mother died, on top of all the
other things we had to do, we had to find a home
for 1,800 shakers. Not so cute.*

In Act 3 adult children can't ignore the stuff in their parents' lives. Downsizing and death will force the issues. So, stop and think: What does your parents' stuff mean to them? What does it say about their values and how they lived? How will you behave toward their stuff when the time comes? An eighty-year-old recalls: "You never forget what it felt like going to bed hungry." We can't imagine, but we can respect the memory. Many of our parents' generation, like Cedric in the story below, grew up during the Great Depression, and as children they had very little.

*Cedric was ten in December of 1933 when his
younger brother was born. He was not only ex-
cited about this new addition to the family, but
also about Christmas just a few days away.
Times were tough on the farm during the Depression. Cedric recalls the somber words of his
father: "Son, your brother is going to be the only
present you'll get for Christmas this year."*

Similarly, many of our parents had very little when they first married. That West Bend waffle maker with the frayed cord you think should be trashed may be a symbolic possession. Its value may be to trigger good memories of how far they've come since they started their lives together. As we grow older, memories appreciate in value.

After you have a better appreciation for what your parents' possessions might mean to them, try to anticipate the potential complexity of the situation you will inherit when the time comes. For example, my mother, the minimalist, travels lightly. My dad, the collector, saves everything. Pack rat parents living in a double-garaged, two-story colonial provide their children a different challenge than parents who have led a Spartan existence and made a downsize move already.

Think worst-case scenario: If your parents died tomorrow, how much of their stuff would you and your siblings be left to deal with? Would you have any idea what should go where? Who should get what? What's of value to family and what's of worth to Goodwill?

Here's your question: "How can I honor and respect the importance of the stuff in my parents' lives *and* do the right thing with it after they're gone?" We can learn from the experience of others.

Older people can become trapped by their possessions. Once they owned their things; now their things own them. They may have reached an age or state of health at which they should be downsizing and moving to a smaller home or a retirement community, but they can't bring themselves to part with a houseful of belongings. They become overwhelmed by the thought of separating, and it becomes a barrier to moving forward. If your parents have decided to move from their home, but a year or more has gone by without them putting it on the market, that's a good sign they're having problems dealing with their stuff.

In some cases, older people can't face the thought of getting rid of their possessions because they know the process of doing so will create conflict in their family over who gets what. They conclude the best way to deal with that problem is not to deal with it, so they remain in a home that becomes a shrine to their inability to make a decision. We've known people who have moved roomfuls of their belongings to storage. "Out of sight out of mind," they say. Storing it is less stressful than deciding who should receive what.

Even when older people do separate and relocate, the transition can carry quite an emotional impact for them and their children, as the following story shows:

> *My mother, Ida, was born on the farm where she and my father, Alvin, spent fifty-five years of their marriage and where I grew up. A tiny lake was near the front porch of the cottage-style farmhouse. As they grew older, Mom and Dad realized they needed to move, so they selected an apartment in town. They couldn't take all of their belongings with them, so with my help, they prepared for an auction sale. I'll never forget the farm auction. In a matter of a few hours, a lifetime of their farming possessions were sold. I detected tears in my parents' eyes. When they sold the old hay baler, I cried too. The money Dad had made from custom hay baling summers long ago had put me through college.*

It's a good idea to approach your parents about dealing with their belongings while they are healthy, have the energy to do so, and can actually have some fun in the process. There's wisdom in the adage "You can't take it with you," so the time will come to remind your parents of that.

Encourage your parents to give some of their treasures away at holidays, birthdays, or anniversaries. Have fun with it. Here's how Pat's Aunt Ethel did it.

> *Aunt Ethel's husband was a compulsive collector and hoarder of antiques. Those he bought at estate sales he stored in a network of garages around town. They had no children. Ethel was left without a pension or a 401k—just buildings full of valuable antiques. Ethel lived by selling piece by piece from the collection to antique dealers from across the country. When Ethel joined her niece Pat's family for family gatherings, she brought little somethings from her collection— items carefully selected to match the interests of each member of Pat's family. Those gifts were appreciated more than anything store-bought, and Ethel delighted in the giving.*

A grandmother chose to give away family keepsakes to each of her two children and seven grandchildren at milestone events in their lives—age eighteen and weddings, for example:

> *Grandma thoughtfully went through her special things, putting each in a gift-wrapped box addressed to one of us. Included with each item was her handwritten provenance of sorts. She wrote of how she obtained the item and why it had special meaning. She gave me her soft leather baby shoes. Today I have the shoes, the note in her hand, and the memory of her thoughtfulness.*

A good way to initiate a caring conversation with parents regarding their possessions can center on your family's cast of characters and their unique needs.

"So, Mom, let's think about who in our family could use some of the things you don't use too often or at all. You know, grandson David could really use the old Ford. What would you think of selling it to him? And Mary's family just bought that cabin up north. I'm sure they could use the bedroom furniture you've stored over the garage."

> *"What a joy for Grandma to give Michael and Tammy furniture from the farm to start their first apartment. Things she loved had a new home with people she loved."*

Though material possessions are lost, the parents gain a sense of control and pleasure in passing on things that are special to them. Giving to family members and friends is preferred because it is more personal than giving to Goodwill, the church rummage sale, or the Salvation Army, although charities are excellent options, and a time for using them will likely come.

And what about your mother's collections? Mindful it

means more to her than anyone else in the family, you owe her a caring conversation that could go like this: "Mom, can we talk about your salt and pepper shaker collection? It's one of a kind. What would you like us to do with it when the time comes? Do you want to keep it intact? Or should we divide it among the grandchildren?" She'll be pleased you cared enough to ask and comforted to know she can make a home for her collection before she goes.

When the time comes to divide possessions among family members, absent a written directive from your parents or their active presence to call the shots, it's important that your family agrees on a methodology that's fair to all. What you devise should be unique to your family. Consider what works, stick with it, and allow enough time to do it right.

Here's an approach that didn't work well—when a sibling charged ahead without consulting others:

> *"My mother told her grandchildren, 'I would welcome you letting me know which things you would like, but don't expect to get everything you want.'"*

> *Betty and her husband, Henry, had lived in the same house for forty years. They were the typical Depression-era survivors in that they were savers. Every square inch of their house had something—usually in boxes. In some rooms things were stacked to the ceiling. Betty and Henry intended to clean things out. They would occasionally go through a box, but it took all day because they held each item and reminisced about it.*

*Even though their children teased them about the situation and offered to come and help them clean and sort, they continued on as they were.*

*As Betty and Henry's health began to fail, their daughter took charge of the situation and started sorting, throwing, and donating much of the contents of the boxes. The remaining siblings felt cheated that they had never had the chance to see what was in those boxes.*

The number of items to deal with can be overwhelming, so it's helpful to make a list (in other words, take inventory) and then divide the items into three categories:

1.  Things that have dollar value: a coin collection, the sterling silverware, the cut glass, or first-edition books, for examples.

2.  Things that are considered family heirlooms: the blanket Grandma quilted in 1902, Grandpa's pocket watch, or the samovar that came over from Russia with the great grandparents, for examples.

3.  Things that have high sentimental value: your baton-twirling trophy from junior high, the family photo albums, or family Bible, as some examples.

After listing the items in these categories, determine a way that's fair to all in your family for dividing them. Fol-

lowing are some ways that families choose to do this. Realize
that you don't have to use the same method for all categories—whatever works best for your family.

One group of siblings de-
cided that they would take turns
selecting items. They drew numbers from a hat that determined
the order in which they selected
items. The oldest sibling had the
honor of drawing first from the
hat. They took turns selecting
one item at a time until all items
were spoken for.

> "I have two children; my
> brother has six. I'll forever
> feel that his family got
> more from my parents'
> estate than their fair
> share, simply because they
> had more children."

Another couple held a garage sale when they sold their
home and moved to a condominium. Everyone—family,
neighbors, friends, and garage-salers—bought what they
wanted at the sale.

In the following story, Janice handled the dispersal of
her parents' possessions with efficiency and tact:

*Janice was one of eight children, and she had
come to help her dad, Chet, move into an apartment. Chet and his wife had lived in the same
house for sixty years and had the usual accumula-
tion that goes with never moving from the family home. Janice took responsibility for cleaning
out the house. She knew that her siblings would
not be able to spend much time helping her, yet
she wanted to make sure they all had a part of
the decision making. She made lists of books and*

*sent them to her siblings so they could select any that might be of interest to them. She took digital photos of other items and sent them via e-mail so her siblings could assist in deciding the fate of their father's possessions.*

> *"My grandmother asked each of us what we wanted. We told her. Privately. Then she made a list and included it with her will. Everything else was given to my mother to dispose of."*

For an estate with a high dollar value, some families have found it helpful to agree in advance how much things are worth and then buy from the estate. This works if all the family members have sufficient funds to buy what they want.

Ideally, your family should still be talking to one another after your parents' items are placed. Although everyone may not feel they got exactly what they wanted, they should feel that the process was fair.

Here's the story of a motivated woman who devised her own inventory categories rather than use the three we suggested:

*It was no surprise to his family when Orville dropped dead at the kitchen table Good Friday evening. It was a shock, but somehow his family always knew he would never move off the farm. When Orville died, he left Myrna with nearly fifty years of rusting farm equipment and all that goes with a dairy farm operation.*

*Myrna was overwhelmed with the suddenness of becoming a widow. There was one thing she knew: she did not want to be on that farm next winter. She took charge and started organizing for the auction sale. As she sorted through sheds and garages she took on the motto, if it's green, it's John Deere; if it's yellow, it's Minneapolis Moline; and if it's orange, it's Allis Chalmers. With the help of her family, she had the auction sale ready to go less than two months after Orville's death and was settled into the house in town within six months.*

We've spoken of the challenges that possessions may introduce, but we close reminding you of their poignancy. After one or both of your parents die, their things become your things either in fact or in memory. There's no rush to cleaning out their clothes closets or going through their photo albums, but you'll likely shed a few tears when you do. Some families agree on a certain day and time to do this together, following a process they've agreed upon. There's therapy in the reminiscing the items will produce. Savor each story; treasure each memory.

---

***Start talking with your folks and family about who should get what, when, and how. Get it done, but keep it fun.***

---

# 9

# PLACE MATTERS

Commonly, our parents continue to live in the communities where they raised their families, grew their friendships, and retired from their work. They stay where things are familiar, where they feel their sense of place, their sense of belonging. They may downsize, but they stay put. Family comes to them.

Many growing-older parents, often soon after retirement, will pack things up and move to select regions of the country that boast year-round tee times, lots to see and do, and relatively carefree living. Other retirees see this as a time in their life to travel. They have spirits for adventure and discovery. Says one adult child,

> *My parents retired, sold everything, bought a giant RV, and hit the open road to visit every national park. I wasn't just surprised; I was stunned. But they're having a blast, and I'll be ready for "the call" when it comes. They even have*

*one of those bumper stickers about spending the inheritance!*

Some cultures build into their expectations that a widowed or frail parent will move in with one of their children, as shared in the following instance. In our increasingly mobile society, this happens, but less often than it used to.

> *Dad was living alone and dying of cirrhosis. I brought him to live with us for his last year. The girls were gone and it was something I could do. The circumstances were not always pleasant, but we got through it, and I think we were all made better by the experience. Dad died surrounded by people who loved him.*

The options are increasingly varied and valid as long as they meet the desires and needs of the persons. Kids are often surprised by their parents' choices. An underlying assumption is that each partner is healthy and able to enjoy life.

When physical and cognitive health issues begin to emerge, however, or one partner dies, the dynamics change and thoughts turn to "home" where healthcare is known and trusted and "the kids are closer."

So, good kids, with good intentions, will probably entertain these questions at some point, if only in passing: *Should we move Mom closer to us? Or in with us?* The answer is: it depends. Some do. Most don't. And for either option, there are good reasons.

In some cases, growing-older parents may be waiting in

*fear* that the question will be asked. In other cases they may be waiting in *hope*. In all cases this is definitely a *Proceed with Caution—Homework Required* situation.

Stop and think even before raising the questions. Candidly think through the motivation for the move and ramifications of the new arrangement. Whose needs are being met? What will it mean to all family members? What do your parents say they need? What do you see them needing? Reconcile the various perspectives and then, after the need is clear, proceed to ponder how best, where best, and who best to meet it, and then begin some caring conversations.

> *"I moved Mother to a charming little apartment in our town. She's unhappy and blames me. What was I thinking? I guess I wasn't."*

Adult children forget how busy their lives are, how quickly their days are filled with pressing activities. The notion that "if mother comes to live in our town or in our house, we will have more time together" is often a faulty notion, given how busy people are.

Much has been written about the various traumas associated with relocation.

Separating from that which is familiar, predictable, and satisfying can be a great trauma at any age, and especially in one's seventies and eighties. Therefore, stop and think. Is your parent the kind of person who enjoys change, is flexible, and has something of a pioneer spirit? If so, he or she might be game for a move to your community to be closer.

Such a person could actually thrive in a setting with other retired people, like a senior housing development or a planned retirement community, where others are in the same boat and have moved for proximity and ease of access to adult children and their families. Ideally, things will work out for you as they did for this adult child:

> *Dad and Mom prized their independence, but they wanted to be part of our lives, too. So they moved into a retirement living center, a contin- uum care place, near my siblings and me. They set up a nice apartment. They made new friends, enjoyed the activities, joined us for church and all the kids' stuff. Dad died knowing Mom was set with family and friends, and safety and security, and all the care and service she could ever need. He was her provider to the very end.*

If, on the other hand, you know your parent to be timid, less inclined to take initiative in new situations, and most comfortable with the familiar, then your loved one may not be a candidate for success in a move. Just be honest in your assessment.

When the topic is broached, it's important to take the time to think through all sides and the expectations of the new arrangement. The older person and the well-intentioned adult child need to be brutally honest about the motivations and capacity for success. Gauging expectations is critical.

Just as you would take a new car out for a test drive, it's a good idea to give trial to the idea of an older parent mov- ing to be closer to adult children. This can be done around extended holiday visits, experiencing regions of the country that are not particularly glamorous at certain times of the year: Minnesota in March, for example.

Sad, but so, there will be situations where parents are not in good health and need nursing care. They have less ability to engage in discussions about a move from home and have less invested in the outcome. It simply won't matter to them.

In this situation, it is common and appropriate to make a move that is more convenient for the adult child. This is true if the older person is now a candidate for assisted living or chronic long-term nursing home care. A visit across town is easier for you to make than a visit across country to manage a parent's illness and failing health.

There are things to think about when you shop for senior housing options that your parent might move to in order to be closer to you. It's important that you learn as much as you can about it as a social setting before you encourage your parent to move. For example, if the vast majority of the people living in the setting are native to the locale and have established cliques in the social milieu, your parent might have difficulty breaking in. In the midst of such a setting, the parent may continue to feel socially isolated. "I don't fit in" is not the feeling you want them to have.

Planned retirement living communities will be able to host your loved one for several days of trial stays before any kind of commitment is required. This is like taking a child on a campus visit to a prospective college and is a good thing to do.

Make a list of those things that are important. For example, if your parent is an avid hobbyist or an ardent bridge player and you learn that his or her favorite activities are not a part of the social fabric of the proposed community, your loved one might not be terribly happy in that setting.

There can be many advantages to the older person and adult children who come together at this stage in life to share proximity. Imagine the joy of grandchildren and grandparents who are able to be present at birthdays, piano recitals, confirmations, and graduations. Consider Mary's experience:

> *We brought Mary's mother, Kate, into our active household of three teenage girls. Grandma Kate had her own room decorated with her things and could easily retreat there when the hubbub of activity in the household became too great. More often, Grandma Kate was very much a part of the girls' lives as they grew up. She's sent them all off to college and was there for their engagements, their weddings, and the births of some of their children. This arrangement, unique in so many ways, was a blessing to all concerned. It was done with love and it was done with great attention to those things that clearly made a difference on both sides.*

There are also examples of failed experiences where adult children, with good intentions but unrealistic expectations, have "seduced" a vulnerable older parent to move so that they can be closer and share in each other's lives. Resentments can build on both sides over little things that cause frustration and result in failed experiences. Promising the land of milk and honey is dangerous. It's important that a trial precede anything that would be a permanent, irrevocable relocation.

As we have talked about in earlier chapters, all parties should understand clearly the nature of relationships going into this particular time. Leaving well enough alone might be the best response. In other words, if you have never had a particularly close mother-daughter relationship, your mother moving nearer to you may not be the thing to do. Or if the move happens, you should not expect the relationship to change dramatically.

Often, little things cause frustration and result in failed experiences with the relocation of an older parent. For example, things that are familiar and predictable are no longer there. There is a new doctor, a new local newspaper; the television and radio stations are not in sync with what they remember. The routine things in their lives such as street names and where items are stocked in their grocery store are totally foreign to them. This would be akin to you taking a job assignment in a foreign country with little preparation and no frame of reference.

Bad situations often occur when the relocated adult parent becomes, by default, dependent on the adult child who invited them or seduced him or her to the new environment with the promise that "we'll have so much time together." Our experience is that the probability for success in such a relocation is greatest when both sides have been totally honest in discussing their needs and expectations of one another and the new arrangement.

Moves work best when older people are relocated from where they are to a setting that is designed for older people and has program service amenities that help with the transition. These settings are good at reestablishing the parents' sense of "I am home here," and they help them become less reliant on the presence or the participation of their adult children.

We close with the story of a move that worked well for an adult child, her father, and her father's best friend:

> *When my terminally ill father informed me that he was "not going anywhere" without his beloved dog, Barkley, I knew that a nursing home was out of the question. My friends questioned my decision to move him and Barkley to my home. They were concerned that caring for my father would be too exhausting and emotionally draining. I have to admit, I had that concern, too. However, I also did not want to spend the next few (seven) months driving the fifty miles to his home in the evenings and on weekends to help out.*
>
> *Was it exhausting and emotionally draining? Yes, sometimes. However, the times that stand out in my mind are not the difficult times. Rather, I remember the times that we played Wheel of Fortune and awarded each other a quarter when one of us was lucky enough to guess the puzzle; the evenings when we shared our popcorn with Barkley and exchanged memories from years past;*

*and the many visits from friends and family who gathered around to laugh and reminisce.*

---

**Moves matter. Look before you leap.**

# 10

# Building a Benevolent Conspiracy

It's true that no one can be with their parents all the time and know everything about their health and security. It's also true that, as our parents grow older, they are often less than candid, less than forthright, less than complete in answering the question "How are you doing?" How many times have we heard an older person say, "I don't want to be a burden," or "I don't want to bother the kids"? So, adult children, nearby or scattered, are well served creating a caring network that we call a "benevolent conspiracy."

In a traditional conspiracy, there's someone people are out to get. It's covert or clandestine. In the benevolent conspiracy, people are out to help, to help

> *"I think about how much pain my mother was in for weeks without any of the five of us knowing just how bad it was (yes, she lied). I now wish that my sister and I had sat down with neighbors, friends, and relatives years ago and set up some type of system where we could have gotten feedback on our mother's functioning."*

you help your parents. Parents are very much engaged in the conversations and decisions, as engaged as they can be and want to be.

We suggest that you develop a benevolent conspiracy whether or not you live in the same community as your parents. You could diagram this conspiracy by drawing four concentric circles on a piece of paper. Write your parents' names in the innermost circle. In the next larger circle, add the names of immediate family members, who are usually the first to join the conspiracy. Within the third circle, note the names of people in your parents' community who can help become your eyes and ears. Your parents' neighbors, their best friends, your old friends still in town, their pastor, the mail carrier, Meals on Wheels, and a local grocery that delivers can help keep an eye on them for you. (We talked about these conspiracy members in Chapter 6, "No One Can Do Everything.")

> *"Having wonderful neighbors makes life much easier for all."*

You would use the outermost circle when your parents move to a care community such as assisted living or skilled nursing, writing in it the names of your parents' nurses, social workers, and administrative leaders. The facility may provide some of the things you relied on family or community members to watch for, so when your parents make such a move, you can update your list of whom you're counting on for what tasks.

There's nothing more trying than long-distance worry about a loved one. You will maintain peace of mind knowing that a caring community surrounds and supports your parents as they grow older. They will be there when you cannot.

Here's when and why Greg decided it was time to form a benevolent conspiracy for his parents:

*On a business trip, Greg, the oldest of his siblings, called his parents, who lived in a small town in Indiana. His dad was at a Rotary meeting, but his mom was home to answer the phone. "How are you guys doing?" His mom said, "Oh, we're just fine," but there was something about her voice that told Greg things might not be "just fine." None of his siblings lived nearby. Greg slept fitfully that night. The next day he called his parents' pastor and one of his dad's best friends to ask each if they would check on his folks. Each did and reported back that things did in fact appear "just fine." Given that assurance, Greg felt much better, but he realized the need to talk with his siblings and create a benevolent conspiracy for the times ahead.*

## Who to Enlist in Your Benevolent Conspiracy?

Who should belong to your benevolent conspiracy? These questions may help you form your list of candidates: Who lives in town with your parents and cares about them almost as much as you do? Who do you trust? Who do your parents trust? Who do they see regularly that could spot changes in

> *"It's important to keep the lines of communication about the parent open between caregivers and adult children."*

their behavior or routines should they occur? Who would you feel comfortable calling and asking to be part of this team?

Call or visit those on your list to ask them to join the conspiracy. Be as specific as you can in what you need from them and share how they can best contact you if the need arises. As time goes by, it's nice to thank them appropriately for what they're doing.

Communication among the caring community you form here and the family members you assigned roles to as outlined in Chapter 6 is extremely important. All should have the most current "what's happening" information related to your parents.

### What Does Your Benevolent Conspiracy Do?

What types of things should you have your benevolent conspiracy watch for? Health and safety concerns are high on the list as well as forewarnings of any of the Big Ds (dementia, drinking, depression, and driving)—topics we discussed in Chapter 7. Financial scams are of growing concern. Also, more older people are using the Internet to manage their retirement portfolios through e-trading and to manage their banking. Some older people inadvertently let their insurance policies lapse. You might ask to be listed on your parents' policies and accounts as a contact to be notified if they miss a premium.

> *"Convincing my mom to join a support group was the best thing that happened. While family and friends were of great help to her during my dad's later years, there was something about the support group that was priceless."*

If anyone in the caring network sees or hears red flags in these areas, ask them to let you know.

How do the members of the benevolent conspiracy watch for these kinds of things? They might drive by your parents' house and see if the mail is getting picked up, the grass mowed, or the sidewalk shoveled. If they see strange cars parked in the driveway, they can investigate. They could call regularly just to say hi, drop by for coffee, or offer your parents rides to appointments. Ideally, the conspiracy sends a message to your parents that says, "We care about you, and it's not a burden doing so."

Here's a situation in which a benevolent conspiracy (the staff at the Assisted Living Center) provided guidance and counsel to the adult children:

> *I began to worry about Mother after a phone call in which she sounded isolated, sad, and even depressed. She seemed okay three months ago when she moved from home to the Fairview Assisted Living Center. I had been calling regularly to check on her, and things seemed fine. After I hung up, I called Martha, the director of nursing at Fairview, and expressed my concern. Martha quickly reassured me, "Oh, your mother's doing just fine. She's sitting in on the book study groups, coming to evening movies every Friday night, and laughing and talking with the staff and residents. She may just be wanting a little more attention from you and your siblings." Given that cue, my brothers and I devised a plan where one*

*of us would stop by to visit her at least once a
week.*

## The Care Facility Staff Members Are Your Friends

A reminder that, if your parent moves to a care facility, their staff is not the enemy. They have a breadth of information and experience caring for many people, so we suggest you trust them and their advice as shown in the following circumstance:

> *Once we accepted the reality of Dad's need for skilled care in the nursing home, we realized his caregivers were not the enemy. They were our partners in keeping our dad safe and clean and fed and loved. They were an extension of us. With that perspective, we were able to share information about Dad's past and his preferences. They welcomed this and used the insights to give even better care to our dad. To make it easier for the staff, we named Sally as the family point person, and she relayed concerns between family and Dad's caregivers.*

Families should appreciate the value of speaking with one voice, literally and figuratively, when they have questions, suggestions, or concerns they want to share with personnel at the parent's care community. They should designate a family member to speak for him or her. Also, they need to attempt to understand the environment in which their parent now lives and how best to work within it.

———

*Make a list of who cares about your parents almost as much as you do. Ask them to help.*

# 11

# THEN THERE WAS ONE

We're in Act 3. Mr. Johnson dies. The houselights go dark. The lights come up onto an all-new scene several months later. Mrs. Johnson is center stage. She looks like the same Mrs. Johnson, but it's not the same Mrs. Johnson. Previously shy, tentative, and retiring, she's just auditioned for the lead in a community play. That can't be the mother we know and love, can it? Are the rumors true that she's dating? How should her adult children react? Shocked or supportive?

A husband and wife over time develop an identity as a couple. You know your parents only as a twosome, so upon the loss of one, you may well be meeting the other as an individual for the first time. Most siblings have talked through, or at least thought about, the "what if Mom goes first" and "what if Dad goes

> *"Since Mom died, I'm getting to know a side of Dad that only Mom knew. I see this as Mom's gift to me."*

first" scenarios, so they have an idea how Mom or Dad will react alone. The discussion among siblings goes something like this: "Dad, in spite of his bravado, is passive, needy, and can't match socks. If he's left alone, we're going to have to run an ad immediately for help for him. Mom, on the other hand, knows nothing about finances. I'll bet she doesn't even know where their checkbook is, let alone how to balance it."

Following the death of one parent, you may see a side of your surviving parent—tender, shocking, or possibly embarrassing—that you didn't expect. "I am the *new* one," says the widow or widower, and the adult children begin to reform their relationships with a person they thought they knew. You may see hidden talents emerge, too, as did this adult child:

> *Dad seemed content to let Mom do all the cook-ing, so we never thought he could boil water. It turns out he learned quite a bit from watching Mom's culinary skills during their many years of marriage, and, wow, can he make a delicious omelet.*

This new person doesn't burst onto stage immediately. Typically, there's a period of mourning and sadness that the family endures for weeks and months after the loss, but at some point in time, the surviving spouse starts to show signs of renewal. Here's the experience of an adult child who saw a "new Mom."

*Dad was a great guy, but a tyrant. He ruled the roost, ran the show, and wore the pants. That was clear to all of us.*

*Mother waited on Dad hand and foot. She even peeled his oranges. No question she loved him, but she was dependent on him to a fault. She looked to him for everything. It's just the way they did the husband-wife thing.*

*When Dad died, we were all certain that Mother would fall apart, withdraw and fade into the woodwork. We figured we would have to take over for Dad to get her through a day. Were we wrong.*

*Mother magically transformed into a modern-day woman—a social butterfly, active and independent. I suppose you could say she had suppressed those skills and abilities over the years given Dad's dominance. For sure, while she grieves his loss, she really enjoys being her own woman. The other day she called my brother to announce she was taking a cruise—"something Dad would never let us do." You go, girl.*

When a parent dies, consider regrouping with your family to update the list of assignments you made in Chapter 6, "No One Can Do Everything; Everyone Can Do Some-

> *"I wish I had really understood how much my mother motivated my father and gave him focus and purpose in life. After her death, it was strange and difficult to watch him try to adjust to not having her around. He seemed lost and depressed."*

thing" and relook at who's part of the benevolent conspiracy you formed in Chapter 10.

What may become apparent soon after a parent dies is how much your parents have been covering for one another. We refer to this as "One Plus One Equals One," or complementary maladies. For example, one parent has 20/20 vision but hears poorly while the other is blind as a bat but can hear a pin drop a block away. Together they do fine. When one dies, the other's difficulties may become more apparent to the family, so you may see some needs that you weren't aware of.

Also, you'll be forging a new relationship with your parent, so try to seek first to understand the situation, listen, communicate, and anticipate all over again. You may experience some frustrating times, but hang in there and be as understanding as you can possibly be. Your parent needs you more than he or she may let on as you navigate these uncharted waters for both of you.

> *"My parents would never go anywhere. I always thought that was my dad's influence. But now I know it's my mom. I always thought she would be willing to do anything, that he was the stick in the mud. But that wasn't the case."*

We worry less about our parents when we have two. But as soon as one of them is gone, there's nobody at their side day in and day out, and things can unfold in unusual ways.

Remain encouraging. Do your best to understand the remaining parent's needs and desires as he or she continues on in life.

*When one of your parents is left alone,*
*what might be the issues?*

# 12

# Oops, Two Again!

Just when you think things have settled down and Dad has adjusted to the loss of your mom, things change. Dad begins seeing someone. Your Act 3 now has a modified cast of characters that may include not only his lady friend but also her adult children and their families. The plot thickens!

Adult children can be justifiably ambivalent about their parent's dating. Janet, an only child, told her mother, "I've been an only child all my life. I'm probably not going to do too well with siblings. If I had wanted a sister, I would have kept my Barbie Doll!"

We overheard the adult children of another family saying, "We just buried our mother; don't stick us with somebody else's." It's healthy to express your feelings to your parent about a new relationship. Say it once. Then, prepare to understand the meaning of the relationship and be supportive.

Sometimes it's easier for the adult children to accept their parent's dating if they knew their deceased parent sup-

ported or encouraged it. Here's how one woman, Jean, communicated her wishes:

> *Two weeks before her fiftieth wedding anniver-*
> *sary, Jean lay dying of liver cancer in the hospital*
> *of her small town. Walter, her devoted husband,*
> *refused to leave her side, so evenings he slept on a*
> *cot by her bed. Family, visitors, and hospital staff*
> *noticed them quietly holding hands, preparing as*
> *best they could for the inevitable. Shortly before*
> *she died, Jean began a conversation with Wal-*
> *ter that caught him off guard. "Walter," she said,*
> *"you've been a wonderful husband. When I'm*
> *gone, I would like you to find another woman.*
> *Don't feel you need to stay single out of respect*
> *for me." As Walter, speechless, began to digest his*
> *wife's words, Jean drew a rumpled sheet of paper*
> *from beneath her pillow. "I'd like you to date," she*
> *said with as much of a twinkle in her eye as she*
> *could muster, "but promise me you won't date any*
> *on this list."*
>
> *Following the memorial service, Walter shared*
> *the conversation with his and Jean's two chil-*
> *dren, but he never shared the list. After a year,*
> *he began dating, most assuredly none who were*
> *off limits!*

"Two again" may or may not imply marriage, but it does
assume a new, meaningful relationship that can often be as

committed as marriage. Many adult children have found that things are less complicated if their mom or dad chooses to live with his or her new love without getting married. This can be touchy, but you might hold back on encouraging them to rush into a marriage if you see potential problems: health, finances, or damage to family relationships, for examples.

> *"They reconnected at their sixtieth high school reunion and were married two weeks later. Elder impulse? That was seven years ago."*

Sometimes a parent will have a firm opinion about re-marriage. Women seem less inclined to want or need to re-marry than men, as evidenced by the following story an adult child shares:

> *My mother is an attractive woman, always dressed well, and has a rather charming manner. I've noticed when we're out shopping or attending church, the widowers look at her with interest and flirt. She seems to enjoy it.*
>
> *"Mom, have you ever thought about marrying again?" I asked cautiously, "because it looks like there could be suitors."*
>
> *Her reply was quick, which meant to me that she had given the idea some thought. "I'll never get married again. It would be just my luck he would have a stroke, and I would be visiting him every day at the nursing home, just like I did with your*

*dad, bless his soul. No, marriage isn't for me; at this age it can get way too complicated. I'll stay happy going with the girls to the Friday Night Fish Fries. You know, playing the field."* That's my mom!

What if your parent begins dating someone you or your siblings don't approve of? Can you think back to your high school years when you were dating someone your parents didn't like? Try to put yourself in your parent's shoes. Our message is, celebrate it. How selfish of you to think it's a disgrace to your parents' marriage. In the following situation, two brothers have a difficult time accepting their father's dating, but Connie helps them see things in a positive light.

*My parents were married for fifty-three years. They were devoted to each other and did every-thing together. When Mom died, Dad didn't seem interested in anyone or anything. He didn't smile much. He started to look old. Maybe he was depressed. For sure, Dad was adrift. When he started seeing a lady friend, my brother, Larry, and I were appalled.*

*Her name was Muriel, a widow. They recon-nected at the funeral of a friend, I think. Larry was really upset. I was frustrated too. Larry insisted that Dad's dating was adolescent and a public insult to Mom's memory. Things were tense.*

*Then Connie, Larry's wife, clued us in. "Grow up, boys! Men are wired to be connected and your dad needs a woman in his life. You should celebrate Muriel and be happy for him. He's happy."*

*Larry and I had it all wrong. Connie was right. Dad and Muriel enjoy each other. Dad's smiling again and that gives us comfort. And I even think if they decide to get married, we'll be cool.*

We tend to glamorize new relationships with, "Oh, isn't it wonderful they've found each other in their twilight years." Many new relationships work out just fine, but some don't. In this story, a daughter lost access to her mother who found a new man in her life:

*A friend of mine's mother married a man who seemed delightful at the time. Her mother was able to travel the world and do other things she had never been able to do, but within three years, he was a controlling tyrant and wouldn't let her do anything without him.*

Here's another story with the same theme:

*After my father died, my mother said she would never marry again. She made my sisters and me promise that we would remind her of this should she ever even consider remarrying. Just a few months later, we were in utter shock when she told us she was dating a wonderful man named Oscar. We reminded her of what she had asked us to promise her, but she wouldn't hear any of it. She was in love, and she was going to follow her heart. She married Oscar a few weeks later. We met his three sons at the ceremony. My sisters and I soon felt that we had lost our mom, because she was no longer interested in our families and us; she was too busy with Oscar. Even our holidays were ruined. We wanted Mom and Oscar to come and spend time with our families and her grandchildren. Instead Mom and Oscar insisted that all of their children and grandchildren convene at their home for Christmas dinner.*

> *"I never expected to be dealing with Dad's sex drive when he fell in love at age ninety-one!"*

Rather than providing "do" or "don't do" advice about your parent remarrying, we share a few questions for your consideration. Suppose your mother is considering marrying a widower, Clarence, who seems in reasonably good health. Here are some things you could talk through with your mother and siblings:

• What happens if Clarence has a debilitating stroke and requires skilled nursing care? ("Mom, what would you want us to do if something happened to Clarence early in the marriage and you ended up being his caregiver? You just went through this with Dad and now you're poised for it to happen again.")

- What role will Clarence's children play in such a situation? (You don't want your mom to bear the full burden of caring for him.)
- Who has medical power of attorney for Clarence?
- Is your mother's last will and testament current? What does she want done with her financial and material assets if she dies before Clarence? Should they be divided among you and your siblings? What, if anything, should Clarence receive?
- Is Clarence's last will and testament current?

Couples remarrying late in life are creating prenuptial agreements more often than they did in the past. These agreements address many of the questions in the previous list.

Remarriages create blended families in which new relationships will need to be established. Sometimes the wedding may be the first time that the children of the bride and groom have met, so the lines of communication among the children may take awhile to form.

You never know when your single parent might form another long-lasting relationship. Be as open, understanding, and supportive as you can, remembering it's your parent's life, not yours.

———

*How would it be if your parent developed a relationship with the potential for marriage?*

———

# 13

# BIGGER THAN THE BLIZZARD

Social isolation and feelings of loneliness are the malnutrition of the elderly. Your parents' worlds shrink gradually as they age, which can result in their living like survivors on a remote island. If they socialize, they may do so only with others of their generation, and they run the risk of becoming out of touch with the world around them. They can wither and die, especially if they perceive they've been set aside from the mainstream of life and that no one cares about them any longer.

Adult children tend to pack as many things into a day as they possibly can, maybe feeling it's how they can get the most out of life. Growing-older parents adopt a reverse philosophy. They seem to make the most of a day by slowing

*"Little things mean so much to my parents—a call, a card, a few flowers or a ride in the countryside."*

down, doing less, and sometimes even doing nothing. Keep in mind that you don't have to overplan their lives.

An older couple was leaving church one glorious Sunday morning. They walked slowly, holding hands, along a walkway lined with trees and flowers. They spotted some especially beautiful flowers, stopped, and leaned over to smell their blossoms. Although this took only a few seconds, a line of church members quickly queued impatiently behind. After a few deep breaths to inhale the fragrance, the man turned to the young couple behind him and said, "Sorry, but it took us a lifetime to learn how to do this."

During your family's Act 3, the time you spend with your parents doing simple, not costly, things can mean the most to them. The material things you give them begin to lose their impact. They just increase their pile of stuff. Rather than things, give them your time, for you'll not have that chance after they're gone.

But time doing what? Let's start with something nearly everyone enjoys—ice cream. You or someone else in your family could take your parents for a ride to the Dairy Queen once a week. You can't imagine how much they'll look forward to this "appointment." They'll enjoy the Blizzard or ice cream cone, but the trip really isn't about the ice cream. It's about the conversations you'll have and their enjoying the scenery during the ride. Your actions speak louder than your words, and taking them for ice cream tells your parents you care about them as much as you do the other things going on in your life.

What goes well with an ice cream cone? A ride, of course.

Andrew tells of a ride with his parents that he never tires of taking:

> *Andrew grew up in a small resort town that fea-*
> *tured a bustling main street, a lakeside band shell*
> *in a shady central park, and vacation homes built*
> *along the shores of the lake. He and his family*
> *loved jumping in their car on summer evenings*
> *and going for the thirteen-mile ride around the*
> *lake. After leaving home, a ride around the lake*
> *was something he took pleasure in doing with his*
> *parents nearly every time he visited. Andrew's*
> *mom died ten years ago, but he and his dad still*
> *take the drive. His father typically won't ask to*
> *do so, but whenever Andrew says, "Dad, how*
> *about a ride around the lake," he always replies,*
> *"Sure!"*
>
> *It takes but half an hour to complete the ride,*
> *but in those few minutes they relive a lifetime of*
> *memories. Andrew dreads the day he'll take this*
> *ride alone. But he will, and when he does, it will*
> *bring back wonderful thoughts of his mom and*
> *dad.*

It's hard for us to realize that sometimes doing nothing with our parents is actually doing something. Quietly sitting with them and listening to their stories may be the best gift you could give them—the gift of your undivided attention. Take those moments to ask them questions about their childhoods, or about your childhood, too. They do appreciate a chance to share meaningful memories. Go through photo albums together. Create a family tree and include facts and stories they remember about your ancestors. Record these conversations with them—even transcribe the conversations. Your family will someday treasure the recordings and writings, and you will likely be surprised at the things you find out, as did Walter in the following story:

> *I was amazed at the things I learned from my dad once I started asking him about the past and listening to his stories. For example, he told me that when he dated Mom, he sometimes took her on boat rides in the hopes that this would impress her, and she'd be won over. I was fascinated to hear him tell the story. Never in my growing-up years did our family go on a boat ride!*

Take your parent to the mall for an hour or two of shopping or attend a grand opening of a new store in town. Find a bench strategically positioned for people watching and sit and observe shoppers come and go. You'll be amazed at how entertaining this can be, and how it provides an experience for your parent to share with their friends.

> *A resident of a retirement community told her friends there about her trip to a new shopping mall. "I had heard you needed to take a nap before going to save up energy for seeing all of it,*

*and they were right. My daughter took me there last week, and I couldn't believe it." The resident didn't buy anything, but she visited a place in town that everybody is talking about. The trip provided something she could share at coffee.*

You might invite your parents to a baseball game. Baseball is a relaxed-pace game that's in no hurry to end. In fact, a game can go into extra innings, an apt metaphor for what we all long for in life.

The next time you're out in public, look for the family on an outing with Grandma or Grandpa, as did John in the following situation:

> *"We learned that everything takes longer, so have patience. Patience when you are going somewhere together, patience when you are sharing a meal, patience when hearing the same story over. Patience! Patience! It's not the destination at those times, it's the journey."*

*While my wife and I entered our favorite restaurant for an evening meal, we encountered three generations of a family readying to leave. The frail grandmother looked sharp in her Burberry scarf and cashmere camel coat, her hair freshly coiffed. She stopped to catch her breath at a booth near the door, then tottered along with a grandson at each arm. The group inched along at her pace, respectful of her maximum speed. All smiled and seemed to be relishing the time together while they waited for Grandma's son to bring the car to the front door.*

As you watch for these moments, you'll be surprised how many you see. Experiencing and even witnessing these times of family togetherness can be quite touching and inspiring

In order to enjoy such times with your parents, we offer these words of advice: *prepare to be patient.* And we share a story by Linda about her mother's relaxed pace:

> *I'm much more like my dad than my mom in terms of motion. I like to get things done quickly. So when I accompanied Mom shopping, I prepared myself for slowing down. Mother looked at everything. She picked up items, touched them, and rubbed material between her fingers. She talked to everyone in the store who would listen about the fabric, about this, and about that. One winter day, Mom and I Christmas shopped in Minneapolis. We were ambling along a skyway when she stopped suddenly and gasped, "Oh, look at that."*

> *She startled me. "What, Mom?"*

> *"Look there," she replied as she pointed to a large, lighted Christmas wreath outside the walkway. Snow was falling. A beautiful icicle had formed in the center of the wreath and light was reflecting on it just so. The scene really was breathtaking, and I'm sure I would have flown right by it without notice had she not been along. We stood*

*for some time to marvel at the wreath. Just the*
*two of us.*

As you do your simple things with your parents, you're sure to become frustrated at times. Rest assured, these feelings are normal, and take heart in these words spoken by a devoted daughter: "I may have lost my patience with Dad, but I never lost my love for him."

---

*Make a date. Take your parent to the Dairy Queen, out for*
*coffee, or to the mall—something he or she will enjoy.*
*You will be glad you did.*

# 14

# The Simply Impossible Parent

We see two types of simply impossible parents: the one who either suddenly or gradually over a short period of time becomes difficult, and the one who has been difficult his or her entire life. Let's discuss the former situation first.

If Mom has been pleasant her entire life and suddenly becomes difficult, it is time for her to see her physician; a medical condition could be the cause. She could be having small strokes, an infection may have set in, or she might be experiencing early signs of dementia. One of the first symptoms families notice with dementia is that their parent becomes suspicious, blaming their family for things they can't remember. "You didn't tell me you were going to do that," or "You hid my income checks," or "I know you stole my coat." (Chapter 7 talks more about dementia, drinking, depression, and loss of driving privileges, each of which could contribute to changed behavior.)

If Mom gets a clean bill of health from her physician and still remains unpleasant, you need to continue to seek to understand. Maybe Mom's mad at the world because she's aging, losing her independence. Maybe she's in pain and either doesn't want you to know it or won't take medication to treat it. Maybe she lost a close friend through death or relocation. Maybe someone has offended her, and she's angry at the way she was treated.

If you can't determine what's wrong, talk with the members of your benevolent conspiracy. Are they noticing the same things you are, or is Mom only angry with you? It may be time for a caring conversation with your parent to let her know what you are seeing and feeling, and that you need her help to understand the situation.

Now for the parents who have been impossible their entire life. We begin with an adult child's confession:

> *I've always been jealous of my friends who seem to have wonderful, fun, and friendly relationships with their parents. I don't. I never have.*

We have encountered impossible parents with whom their children have had little chance of forming loving relationships. There are parents who don't want to have a thing to do with their children and those that want them in their presence only so they can manipulate them. We've seen the full range of parental behavior: those who blame, those who demand, those who play favorites, those who are passive-aggressive, and those who are paranoid. We're sorry if your relationship with your parent isn't what you hoped, but please don't give up.

*Once a parent always a parent* seems to be one thing that often frustrates adult children. We knew a ninety-three-year-old man who scolded his son, a prominent and highly respected man in the com-

> "I called Mom to tell her I loved her, and she hung up."

munity, for wearing shorts when he came to visit. "It's inappropriate behavior," said the father. "Men shouldn't wear shorts in public." The son left nearly every visit with a reminder of how he was failing to live up to his father's expectations.

If you're dealing with an impossible parent, it helps to keep in mind that there are no perfect families, no perfect parent-child relationships. A family that may appear idyllic to others may have much internal strife. Remember: all that glitters is not gold. Also, even the most wonderful parent-child relationships have some issues that the parents and children have had to manage.

Your parent may be one who we call *the street angel and the house devil*—those parents who are saints to everyone in the world except their own children. Here's an example:

> *Virginia attended a ninetieth birthday party for a longtime friend. The friend's daughter, Lisa, flew home to attend the celebration. During the fun and festivities, Virginia said to the daughter, "Oh, Lisa, it must be great to be here with your*

*mom. She's such a wonderful lady. My family adores her."*

*Lisa paused for a second, not sure what to say, but then she replied, "You know, it's interesting to hear people talk about my mom. I don't see her that way at all. You and I don't know the same person."*

We've seen other instances where the parent isn't a devil at home, but rather isn't home at all. For our parents' generation, the men were typically the ones making the living while the women worked at home, and some dads became workaholics, committed every waking hour to

> *"My dad was a classic workaholic. I never really knew him. He was always too busy working."*

their jobs, and therefore never developed a relationship with their children. In the following story, George tells of such a situation:

*George attended a memorial service for an eighty-year-old longtime friend at which a few of the deceased's colleagues shared eulogies that spoke of his greatness as a scholar, physician, and beloved man. The stories were tender and touching; they brought tears of sorrow and laughter to many in attendance. Following the service, George said to the man's son, "Weren't those lovely tributes to your father?" He looked at George almost apolo-*

*getically and said, "Yes they were. I wish I had*
*known the man of which they spoke."*

What can you do when you're in the middle of a situation that you feel helpless to change? One thing is to adjust your expectations. If Dad has been negative his entire life, don't be surprised by his negativity. Remember, too, that you can only do what you can do. You and your dad likely didn't develop your current relationship overnight. You may bear some responsibility for the situation, but it has probably been a joint journey. Focus your efforts on how you can be the best child you know how to be in this situation. Your difficult parent may be ready to let go of one or more issues that strain your relationship. If so, are you ready for a caring conversation about them?

*Frank's daughter Linda, one of his five children,*
*married Nat, an African American man. Linda*
*and Nat lived happily together and raised two*
*beautiful children. Frank made it clear that Nat*
*was not welcome in his home, and when Linda*
*visited with her children, Frank ignored them, his*
*own grandchildren. At age eighty-five and after*
*fourteen years of shunning his daughter's family,*
*Frank experienced a change of heart. He began*
*attending the grandchildren's sporting events.*
*He welcomed them and Nat to family gather-*
*ings at his home. It took years, but he changed.*
*Our message is: never abandon your hopes and*
*dreams for loving family relationships.*

A good lesson learned is, don't let others dictate to you their definition of "a good daughter." Your mom's church circle or coffee klatch friends may say, "Well, if Mary Ann were any kind of daughter at all, she'd be up there visiting her mother every Tuesday." They may likely see only your mom's out-in-public side, and that personality may be exactly opposite of what you've had to contend with throughout your life. So they don't understand the entire picture, and if they did, they would see why you're not there every Tuesday.

If you don't have a healthy relationship with your parent, you might ask yourself, who does? You could still, behind the scenes, create a benevolent conspiracy for your parent that includes his or her friends and colleagues, even if you don't have the warm relationship that they do. Be open with these people about your relationship with your parent. Explain the situation as best you can so they understand your point of view and know what they can (and can't) expect from you. They may not need to know all the details of why you "love dad but can't stand to be around him," but it's important that they know you love and care about him.

Also, keep the lines of communication open with your siblings. Just because your relationship with your parents is strained, it need not be so with them. They may have similar issues. If your parent is relying on them, let them know how much you appreciate what they're doing and offer to help them in any way you can.

When dealing with any parent, but especially an impossible parent, be sure to let them know your priorities: your marriage, your children, your career, and your own mental health. Your parents are important, but they need to realize that they aren't the only concern in your life. Also, if they make demands, be truthful in your response to those you will and won't accept. Your parents may not like your positions, but at least they will know what they are. It's okay to hold firm.

Finances can often be a source of tension among aging parents and family, even when relationships are good. If your parent is generally impossible, it's best that you leave management of his or her finances to a third party: a trust officer, banker, personal investment manager, or attorney. This person can make monthly or quarterly statements available to ensure that finances are being adequately managed. If your parent's giving or loaning money to family members has become a sore point, the third party can address the situation more objectively than family members.

For some adult children dealing with a difficult parent, professional counseling can provide a valuable perspective and help gauge expectations. Realistically, when Mom has been impossible for a lifetime, the only option you may have remaining is to say, "Here's my phone number," walk away, and let be what will be. You aren't being abusive, you're not being neglectful; you've just put your mom in charge of her own destiny when she's proven to be simply impossible. Take comfort in knowing that you are justified in stepping aside. You are justified in doing nothing.

We realize not all relationships end happily and not all unfinished business gets resolved by the time your family's Act 3 ends. After the curtain falls, however, you want to be able to say, *I honestly tried everything I could think of to better the relationship.* If you truly believe that, you should have no regrets after your parent is gone. You may be sad for not hav-ing a relationship you had hoped for, but at least you won't feel guilty that you didn't make the effort. Learn from this experience and apply it to your own Act 3.

———

*If your parent is impossible,*
*consider changing your expectations.*

# 15

# AS THE CURTAIN FALLS

Now that you've read this far, you should know more about helping parents grow older than the person sitting by you on the plane or standing with you at the supermarket checkout. We hope the insights we've shared have not only informed and touched you, but have also motivated you to proceed.

So what will you do with the time remaining in your family's Act 3? For a starter, get your family working together on a plan to support your parents through their growing-older years. Initiate caring conversations. Take charge and guide your family's Act 3 to a happy ending.

Families commonly have rifts, or fallings-out, or estrangements, even schisms. Someone did something or didn't do something, someone said something or didn't say something, and it starts. Intense feelings of anger and animosity fester and good

> *"I know it was a big deal (becoming mad at one another years ago), but I can't honestly remember why. Different things are important now."*

people behave poorly. It ranges from the suppressed, unspoken to the classic Hatfield and McCoys. We refer to these dynamics as "family hatchets" and strongly suggest they be buried in your Hatchet Cemetery before the final scene of Act 3.

Imagine how difficult it is for the estranged sibling to rejoin the family at a time of parent crisis or at the time of dying and death. Reason enough to bury the hatchets. What would be inscribed on the tombstones in your family's Hatchet Cemetery?

> *Here lies John's anger toward his father for never speaking words of affection or pride.*

or

> *Here lies Jack's jealousy of Tom's business success.*

or

> *Here lies Amy's frustration with her mom for never accepting the man she married.*

We've heard too many sad stories of parents and children who have refused to speak, and the silence follows them to their grave. The child lives on with regret that he or she didn't initiate an action that could have resolved the matter. Things need to get resolved, so that peace may come.

In the Judeo-Christian tradition, children are instructed to *Honor your father and your mother, so that you may live long*

*in the land the Lord your God is giving you.* Genesis 20: 12
(NIV). This commandment is the only one of the ten that
promises something in return to those who follow it. It promises that if you honor your parents, *your* days will be long and
things will go well. We're not suggesting that you treat your
parents lovingly solely for selfish reasons. Rather, because it
is the right thing to do and you'll have fewer regrets.

While your Act 3 unfolds, your children are observing
how you treat your parents. After your parents die, their Act
3 ends, and a new Act 3 begins, one in which you will play
the role of the aging parent. If your children have observed
you treating your parents well, they will be more likely to
treat you in a way you prefer.

Each family's Act 3 ends uniquely. Like snowflakes, no
two curtains fall in exactly the same way. Though we can't
always script the ending to our liking, we may have more
control than we think. An adult child tells how his family
planned a fond farewell for their mother:

> *Four weeks before our mother died, we didn't
> know it was four weeks before our mother died.
> Mother had just completed a round of intense
> chemotherapy for her cancer. My sister, Martha,
> believed Mother was strong enough to enjoy a
> weekend in Chicago. My three brothers and I
> agreed.*
>
> *Martha holds an executive position in her com-
> pany. She called Mom to say, "Mom, I have a
> speaking engagement in Chicago. You're feeling*

*better, why don't you come with me? I'm staying at a lovely hotel on Michigan Avenue. We'll do the weekend up right. You can get some needed rest, too. We'll even have room service." Mom said yes.*

*A limo met Mom and Martha at the airport and whisked them to their downtown hotel. The bellboy escorted them to their suite on the top floor. Martha could almost read Mom's thoughts: "My daughter must really be important if she is treated like this." As they dressed for dinner, there was a knock at the door. "Who could that possibly be?" asked Mom.*

*"I have no idea." said Martha. "I'm not quite ready. Can you get the door?"*

*Mom opened the door to see me and my brothers dressed to the nines in tuxedos, beaming with smiles and extending a bouquet of roses.*

*That weekend was all about Mom. She was the queen! We wined and dined and squired her around Chicago. We shared many memories and a few tears. It was perfect. Four weeks later, we buried our mother.*

Fast forward to the day of your parent's funeral or memorial service. How will it be? Friends and family will be gathered. Favorite flowers and songs and readings will be shared. Words of comfort, appreciation, and celebration will be spoken. How will you do?

The best you can hope for is that at the close of your family's Act 3, during the service, you will experience a calm peace of mind and hear a whisper within you: *As I say goodbye, I have no regrets.*

No regrets. There's no better way for the curtain to fall on your family's Act 3.

*Now, put the book down. Call your parents and your siblings, and start the conversations. You'll be glad you did.*

# CURTAIN CALL

Now you know. There are no recipes, no surefire formulas, no "seven-easy-steps" for growing older with your loved ones. It's an experience unique to your family.

We have provided you with some insights and perspectives, some tools and techniques for navigating the journey. Find comfort and reassurance in the experiences of others. Within your family, nurture existing relationships, leverage your strengths, and manage your weaknesses. Stop and think and start the conversations. Evaluate, anticipate, communicate, navigate, and celebrate.

When the curtain falls on your Act 3, you will have done just fine.

-------

*Step back. Assess your family's situation.*
*Work with what you know and have.*

-------

# Our Invitation

Helping our parents as they grow older is a journey we can travel better together.

Please join us at www.momdadcanwetalk.com:

To *comment* on the book's value to you

To *order* additional copies of the book

To *talk* with the authors

To *share your* experience with others

To *ask* your questions

To *receive* a book discussion leader's guide

To *invite* the authors to speak to your group

We look forward to hearing from you.

Dick, Ruth, and Mike

# About the Authors

**Dick Edwards** has thirty-five years of experience working closely with older adults and their families. For the past twenty years he served as administrator of Charter House, a nationally recognized model for excellence in retirement living and long-term health care affiliated with the world-renowned Mayo Clinic in Rochester, Minnesota. At Charter House, Dick was known for his personal interest in staff, residents, and their families, and for his accessibility as they sought his support and counsel. At Mayo Clinic, Dick conducted early research on the question, *Who does better at the business of growing older?*

Dick served in the leadership of the American Association of Homes and Services for the Aging (AAHSA), an organization of six thousand not-for-profit providers of older adult services. He served on the board of directors, led the organization's national quality initiative, Quality First, and was in involved in the early development of the Center for Aging Services Technologies (CAST). For fourteen years,

Dick served in the leadership of Aging Services of Minnesota (ASOM), a statewide association of not-for-profit providers of services for older adults. His excellence in leadership has been honored by Mayo Clinic, AAHSA, and ASOM.

Dick has consulted and lectured throughout the United States and abroad on topics related to (1) growing older and (2) quality service to the needs of persons as they age. His professional reputation is that of a passionate visionary and an articulate, compassionate advocate for persons growing older and their families.

Mr. Edwards is a graduate of Luther College in Decorah, Iowa, and Case Western Reserve University, Cleveland, Ohio. He and his wife, Pat, have three adult children and six grandchildren.

**Ruth Weispfenning** is a licensed social worker and has served for twenty-three years as director of resident services at Charter House in Rochester, Minnesota. In her position, Ruth coordinates new resident orientation and welcoming events and provides ongoing support and counseling services for residents and their families. Building relationships of respect and trust with residents and families, and understanding the unique dynamics of each resident's situation, is essential in her position. Ruth has additional experience in older adult services including therapeutic recreation and fitness, spiritual care, and long-term care. She is a graduate of Moorhead State University, a certified aging services professional (CASP), and a licensed nursing home administrator. Ruth and her husband, Jim, have four grown children.

**Mike Ransom** majored in math at Iowa State University, but the English professor's A+ on a paper he wrote planted the seed that he might have a knack for writing. He joined IBM in 1970 and worked for them first as a technical writer and then as a manager of various departments until he retired in 2000. From his IBM experiences, Mike learned much about working with people, managing large projects, assimilating vast amounts of information, and communicating it clearly to its intended audience. In 1997, Mike completed a book about his grandparents that changed his life. Since that experience, he has written fourteen memoirs for clients, nearly all in their eighties or nineties; published twenty-two personal profile articles in a regional magazine, *Generations of TODAY;* completed several corporate and family newsletters; and taught workshops that help others write their memoirs. Mike and his wife, Jeanine, have a son, Ben.

Printed in the United States
149373LV00002B/56/P